The Journey Inward

The Journey Inward

A Path to Discovery, Determination, and the Value of Friendship

A Camino Memoir

Janet Charbonneau

Copyright © 2018 Janet Charbonneau

ISBN-13: 978-0-9980370-0-4

All rights reserved. No part of this publication may be reproduced or transmitted in any form or by any means, electronic or mechanical, including photocopy, recording, or any other storage and retrieval system, without permission in writing from the publisher.

Front Cover Photos: Janet Charbonneau and Jay Schwantes
Back Cover Photo: Janet Charbonneau
Cover Design: Klassic Designs
Interior Map Design: Jay Schwantes

Published by:
Janet Charbonneau
PO Box 80343
Charleston, SC 29416

www.TheJourneyInwardBook.com

This book is dedicated in loving memory of my Dad and my two brothers, Den and Paul. My Dad taught me the value of independence, while my brothers taught me to have a sense of adventure. Thank you for giving me the strength and determination which has allowed me to experience such amazing adventures.

Table of Contents

Acknowledgements xi
Introduction 1
Preparation 14
The Adventure Begins 33
Pamplona to Muruzabal 40
Muruzabal – Villatuerta 48
Villatuerta – Los Arcos 55
Los Arcos – Logrono 62
Logrono – Najera 70
Najera – Santo Domingo 73
Santo Domingo – Belorado 77
Belorado – San Juan de Ortega 80
San Juan de Ortega – Burgos 85
Burgos – Hornillos del Camino 89
Hornillos del Camino – Castrojeriz 92
Castrojeriz – Boadilla del Camino 98
Boadilla del Camino – Villacazar de Sirga 102
Villacazar de Sirga – Calzadilla 104
Calzadilla – Sahagun 108
Sahagun – Reliegos 112
Reliegos – Leon 115
Leon – San Martin del Camino 122

San Martin del Camino – San Justo	125
San Justo – Rabanal	132
Rabanal – Molinaseca	139
Molinaseca – Cacabelos	146
Cacabelos – Ambasmestas	149
Ambasmestas – O Cebreiro	155
O Cebreiro – Triacastela	159
Triacastela – Sarria	164
Sarria – Portomarin	170
Portomarin – Palas de Rei	176
Palas de Rei – Ribadiso	179
Ribadiso – Arca	182
Arca – Santiago	185
Muxia and Finisterre	192
Santiago	194
Santiago – Madrid	196
Madrid – Charleston	198
Epilogue	200
Appendix A	215
Order Your Custom Map Today!	219
Thank you!	221
About the Author	223

Acknowledgements

Thank you to all of my friends and family for supporting me during my walk. It was the toughest thing I have ever accomplished, and the encouragement was invaluable!

A sincere thanks to Diane Bock for being an awesome hiking buddy. She did most of the navigation which I greatly appreciated. She was fun, and we had interesting discussions on all aspects of life. I am grateful to have hiked with her!

A heartfelt thank you to my Mom for never telling me that my adventures are crazy and for passing on the stubborn gene to me. That stubbornness has allowed me to accomplish my amazing goals!

For the rest of my family, thank you for supporting me in my wild adventures and cheering me on along the way every time.

Many thanks to all my reviewers for reading my book and giving me priceless feedback to help me improve it. A special thanks to the reviewers who participated in more than one review! With each review phase, it let me know that I was moving in the right direction and gave me feedback on areas that needed more description and feelings. Thank you for the grammar corrections as well. Grammar is extremely important to me since I stumble over grammar errors when I read other books. Mary Ann Tormey did a wonderful job as my final grammar reviewer.

Here is a list of my reviewers (in alphabetical order) and their relationship to me.

Reviewers:

- Diane Bock – My Camino hiking buddy
- Fran Charbonneau – My Mom
- Radeen Cochran – Friend from my sailboat adventures

- Wayne Collins – Co-worker, manager, and mentor
- Kathi Dubuque – Friend from a networking group in Charleston, SC
- Kathy Hart – Previous neighbor in Willow Springs, NC
- Pam King – My best friend in Charleston, SC
- Jean Kurpiel – My cousin
- Blaine Parks – Ex-husband, mentor, and cheerleader
- Nancy Radcliffe – Friend from the Grateful Goldens Rescue
- Suzanne Redmond – Friend from my Camino adventure
- Julie Thorington – Friend from my Hogs for Dogs adventure
- Mary Ann Tormey – Friend from my early childhood
- Nancy Walter – My cousin

As you can see, my reviewers came from all aspects of my life, including my numerous diverse adventures. I am grateful for having such a wonderful support group for my book writing endeavors!

A special thank you to Jay Schwantes for creating the map of my Camino journey that appears at the beginning of this book. He supported us during our Hogs for Dogs adventure by designing and hosting our website along with being on our Board of Directors. He has wonderful creative talents which you can see in my Camino map as well as at the end of my book where I have an example of Camino maps that he can custom design for your Camino journey. Please check out the "Order your map today" section at the end of this book or go to www.aroadtosantiago.com for more details.

My deepest gratitude to Blaine Parks for not only being a reviewer but in assisting me with the many facets of the publishing and marketing process. He showed me how to design my website and helped me with the marketing process. He also assisted me in reviewing all the book cover designs and suggested changes to improve the designs. He was my cheerleader, propelling me forward when I stalled in the writing, editing, publishing and marketing processes. Thank you for the endless support!

For my book cover design, I used 99designs.com and I would highly recommend them. I created my design contest and had numerous designers who submitted designs. I used the polls to request votes and comments from my friends and family which gave me invaluable feedback. It was a wonderful experience!

Thank you to the amazing designer, Klassic Designs, who won my contest on 99designs.com. He was awesome in how quickly he responded to my feedback and requests. From the very first design entry he submitted, I fell in love with the design of the title. Per my request, he then added my own pictures to the cover design. He beautifully orchestrated a combination of two of my Camino pictures for the front cover. He used a picture of a rocky path to represent my past life journey as well as a picture of one of the towns I passed through on the Camino to represent my Camino journey. A picture from Jay Schwantes was also used for the Camino marker. Klassic Designs expertly meshed those pictures together to create my incredible front cover design which represents my journey.

For the back cover, Klassic Designs used my picture of a lone tree that was taken as I walked through the Meseta during my Camino. It represents me, single and strong, after I finished my Camino. I love the cover as it is beautiful and symbolic of my life. Klassic Designs also created bookmark designs for me to use for the two-sided bookmarks that I am using for marketing. I am thrilled with how amazing they turned out. I highly recommend Klassic Designs on 99designs.com for any of your design needs. He provides excellent customer service! I look forward to working with him in the future!

Lastly, thanks to my sweet Golden Retriever, Holly, who sat near me and gave me wet kisses on my nose when I stressed over the book process. She was a well-needed comfort. I love that girl!

The entire process, including initial writing, edits, publishing, and marketing, was a difficult learning experience, but I am grateful to my support team of family and friends who have been there every step of the way.

CAMINO
DE SANTIAGO

CAMINO FRANCÉS
"THE WAY OF SAINT JAMES"

FRANCE

SPAIN

PAMPLONA

BURGOS

THE MESETA ⊢ ALTO DE PERDON

Introduction

I sat there staring at my bucket list as my 50th birthday loomed before me. It was three months before my birthday and there I sat with absolutely no plans. I was not about to let my milestone birthday slip by with no exciting celebratory plans on the calendar! I started to think of crazy ideas for a birthday trip, so I had pulled out my bucket list for inspiration. Since I didn't want to depend on having someone else join me, it needed to be something that I could do solo. What could I do that was out of the ordinary and that I was willing to take on solo?

Many people have a bucket list of things they want to accomplish before they die and I was no exception. There were several items on the list that I had already accomplished, but many more sat on the list waiting to be achieved. I scanned the list to see which ones were still waiting to be checked off.

Janet Charbonneau

Bucket List:

- Get a Bachelor of Science degree in Computer Science - check
- Go whale watching - check
- Travel through Europe - check
- Travel to Australia
- Travel to New Zealand
- Travel to Ireland
- Travel to Scotland
- Travel to Iceland
- Get married - check
- Live on a sailboat – check
- Swim with dolphins
- Fly on a seaplane
- Take an Alaskan cruise
- Learn to ride a motorcycle – check
- Ride a motorcycle across the US - check
- Travel to all 50 states – 48 down, Hawaii and Alaska remaining
- Publish a book
- Go skydiving
- Hike the Camino de Santiago
- Fly in a helicopter

My completed bucket list items showed that I was certainly no stranger to adventure and ideas that family and friends thought were crazy. Right after graduating from college, I took four weeks off to tour through several countries in Europe. Since I was just about to start a new job and I didn't know when I would be able to get that much time off again, it seemed like the perfect time to explore Europe. My childhood friend, Stacy, and I traveled to England to visit

The Journey Inward

Cambridge and London before joining up on a bus tour through England, France, Luxembourg, Belgium, Netherlands, Germany, Austria, Switzerland, Italy, and Greece.

In 2000, my husband, Blaine, and I sold our house in Willow Springs, NC and moved onto a 40' sailboat with our two Golden Retrievers, Max and Bailey. It was extremely difficult since we were selling our dream house that included 5½ acres and a pond. We had picked out the lot and house design and had the house built to our specifications. We loved this house, along with the awesome wrap-around porch.

Not only was it our dream house, but it was also our house in which we created all of our dreams. Finishing the house and moving into it accomplished our first dream together. It was where we learned to follow our dreams and not let anything get in our way. It is also where we learned to not take "NO" for an answer. We tried to purchase a new Beneteau sailboat as our first sailboat and were turned down for the financing. That just made us work harder on our goal.

We had a goal of buying a boat and retiring on it. It had been a dream of Blaine's for many years and I fell in love with the idea when he told me about it. When we got married, it became a goal for both of us. We weren't going to let anything stop us from achieving that goal. Not too long afterward, we managed to purchase a used Island Packet 35. It was a boat built to cruise around the world. Not being able to purchase the Beneteau ended up being a blessing since the Island Packet was one that I liked even more than the Beneteau. We were one step closer to our goal.

An aggressive savings strategy along with Blaine's stock options with Cisco Systems allowed us to retire earlier than originally planned. We were able to buy a brand new Island Packet 40 sailboat and outfit it for blue water cruising. It was unbelievable to be able to retire at age 35 on a brand new sailboat. We couldn't believe that, after only five years of being married and moving into this dream house, we were able to quit our jobs and move onto our sailboat.

Janet Charbonneau

Our neighbors were amazing and we were going to miss living there. Since we were the first ones to move into our new subdivision, we had greeted each new neighbor as they moved in. We had a yearly pig pickin' where we invited all of our neighbors, along with friends and family. We made our subdivision into a very friendly neighborhood. It broke our hearts to leave these wonderful friends behind, but we knew that friendships would survive the distance.

We sold or donated most of our material possessions. We kept a couple pieces of furniture that would be used by my sister, some kitchen and dining room pieces and our memories captured in photos and scrapbooks. Everything else that could not go on the boat with us was sold. It was scary to part with all these items that we had spent years collecting. What if sailing didn't work out and we needed to move back into a house? What would it be like to start all over again?

After working many years at IBM during the business suit era and the last couple of years at an IT consulting business, I had a plethora of business suits, skirts, and dresses. I wasn't planning to wear any of those again, so I donated all of my business clothes to a women's charity who helped abused women escape their current situation and start over. I was grateful to be able to help these women start their new life as I started my new life as well.

We spent months clearing out the house and many weekends holding garage sales to sell everything. It was heartbreaking to see the items you loved being sold for a few dollars or less.

We had been planning this for five years. Modifications were made to the boat that allowed our two Golden Retrievers to be able to sail with us. We were fortunate to be able to quit our jobs and cruise full-time for 3½ years. While many cruisers traveled the East Coast of the US via the safety of the Intracoastal Waterway, we usually traveled via offshore routes. This allowed us to explore the east coast of the US, Nova Scotia, and the Bahamas.

The Journey Inward

If quitting my job, selling almost everything I owned, and setting sail for foreign ports wasn't crazy enough, I also spent seven months in 2004 riding a motorcycle with my Golden Retriever, Bailey, in my sidecar. Blaine had an identical rig with our other Golden Retriever, Max, happily cruising along in his sidecar.

I had only been a passenger on a motorcycle a couple of times in my life and had never ridden one by myself. The preparations included taking a motorcycle riding course, starting out on a smaller motorcycle for practice, and eventually moving up to a Harley-Davidson Ultra Classic with a matching Harley-Davidson sidecar. Many experienced male motorcyclists told me they wouldn't even attempt to ride a sidecar rig, so it was an intimidating endeavor to plan to ride 25,000 miles on that rig. It was quite the challenge, but I had fun preparing for the trip.

We created a non-profit charity called Hogs for Dogs and rode through all lower 48 states raising money and awareness for service dogs. I had learned about service dog organizations in 1990 and had contributed to one of them for many years. I was excited to be able to attract attention with our dogs in sidecars and then spread the word about the independence that service dogs can give to those with disabilities.

Through internet and email, we managed to have events planned for us along our route. We had our dogs certified as therapy dogs; therefore, we were able to stop in schools along the way to teach the students about service dogs and to allow them to meet Max and Bailey. We attended many fundraising events where the dogs attracted attention, which allowed us to talk to everyone about service dogs.

We spent 218 days on the road with just what we could carry in our two motorcycle rigs and stayed in motels or with family, friends or other volunteers. We traveled almost every day and had to navigate unknown territory on a daily basis. Since we had determined that I would always ride in front of Blaine, I became the navigator. GPSs were not that advanced back then, so I had to plan our route and download maps to the GPS every evening. It was extremely stressful making sure we made it to our destination each day without getting lost in the process.

The experience was definitely a challenge, but I thrived on the adventure. Not only was I the navigator for the trip, but I was also the treasurer. I managed the finances and kept track of every donation by the state where it was donated, calculated down to the penny. While Blaine was the big picture guy, I was the details person. Many times it was very daunting to manage the daily finances and other details. We managed to raise over $100,000 and were able to make sizable donations to several service dog organizations because of the ride. I felt this was an amazing feat since it was done before social media was popular.

With these bucket list items completed, I needed another one that would be worthy of a 50th birthday celebration. I wanted to skydive, but skydiving didn't seem as great a challenge as I would like for my 50th birthday. I wanted something that would last longer than one day. There wasn't enough time or money to plan a trip to Australia, so I continued down my list. I was supposed to go on an Alaskan cruise, but my plans fell through, so that would stay on my list for another day. A trip to Ireland or Scotland would be fun, but I thought that I would enjoy it more if someone accompanied me.

Since there were only three months until my birthday, I needed to plan quickly. My eyes skimmed through the list for something that would be a challenge, possibly even out of my comfort zone, but could be accomplished solo if I couldn't find anyone to join me in my crazy adventure. I wanted it to be out of the ordinary and memorable. Then my scan stopped at the perfect 50th birthday celebration: Hike the Camino de Santiago.

My thoughts went back to the time I put this item on my bucket list. I had just finished watching a movie called *The Way* starring Martin Sheen. It was about a man living a somewhat stagnant life

The Journey Inward

who goes to St. Jean Pied de Port, France, to identify and pick up the remains of his son who died the first day out while hiking the Camino de Santiago. While there, he decides to hike the Camino in honor of his son, sprinkling the cremated remains along the way. During his journey, he makes the acquaintance of three people who were from very different backgrounds from him and they end up hiking with him. He forges deep relationships with these new friends and discovers things about himself through those relationships.

It was an intriguing movie. Hiking through the country and stopping at little villages along the way sounded exciting. The relationships that could form during that time were something I had missed from my sailing days. I had never been hiking before, so that would be a physical challenge. Spending all that time hiking appeared like it could be a mental, soul-searching challenge as well. It definitely looked like a life-changing experience, so I had added it to my bucket list.

Like the character in the movie, I felt my life was stagnant. I reflected back on the ten years since we had finished our motorcycle ride to figure out how I had gotten this way. As the years flashed before my eyes, the pain, loneliness, fear, and insecurity came rushing back into me. After finishing our motorcycle ride across the US, we had to figure out what to do next. Since the stock market was booming when we moved onto our boat, we had foolishly kept our investments in the stock market. With the harsh downturn in the stock market in 2001 and 2002, we had watched our investments dwindle. We knew we would eventually have to go back to work since we had not paid off our boat mortgage.

We decided to go into business with Blaine's brother out in Mississippi. He owned a very small car audio business, but it was located in one of the fastest growing towns in the US. We temporarily moved out there to expand the business from a small garage hidden behind a strip mall to a storefront in that strip mall with an installation garage behind it. We invested in the business by setting up the new store. We painted it, set up a checkout counter and bought displays for all of the equipment. We purchased a lot of inventory to put on the new displays and keep in stock.

Once we had opened the new store, organized the business processes and had a profitable business running, we moved back onto our sailboat. The plan was to sail 9 months out of the year and then run the business for three months every summer so that his brother and his wife could take the summer off to spend quality time with their two children.

While the plan worked well in theory, the reality was that his brother and his wife were not capable of properly managing a business. His brother ran up our credit card debt purchasing merchandise for the store. His brother's wife horrendously mismanaged the finances!

After less than two months of watching their actions from afar, we decided that we needed to go back out to Mississippi to get the business back in order. We were sitting at a marina in Charleston, SC where we had stopped to visit with Blaine's parents. Frustrated at the gross mismanagement of the business, we decided that we would move the boat back up to Oriental, NC where we had kept the boat before we went cruising. A friend of ours had offered us their boat dock to moor our boat since we didn't know how long we would be out in Mississippi.

Unfortunately, when we got to the store in Mississippi, his brother had changed the locks; thus, he locked us out of the business we shared. We were livid and ended up hiring a lawyer to shut down the business. After a few months of battling between the lawyers, we still had no luck in shutting down the business. It continued until his brother ran out of money and couldn't pay the rent for the store. He took everything that was still in the store and then sold it for his profit. Sitting in a pile of debt, we had to find a plan B to find new income.

Blaine decided he wanted to start a marine services and yacht delivery business. We wanted to find a town with a booming boat

The Journey Inward

population so he could have plenty of boat maintenance jobs as well as a good airport to be able to fly in and out of for the yacht deliveries. We discussed different towns from Virginia to Florida and decided on Charleston, SC.

Once Blaine had his business started, it was time for me to find a new job. Since Charleston was a tourist destination, it was overflowing with restaurants. I decided to try out bartending for a while. After two months of bartending at a chain restaurant and another month of looking for another bartending job, I stumbled across a job ad that tossed me into the car business.

After three months of crazy hours working at a Toyota dealership, my marriage started falling apart. We had been able to work through our problems in the past, but this time it just blew up out of control. After many deep discussions, we realized there was no way we could resolve our issues. I wanted to move off of the boat, but had just moved from floor sales to internet sales at the Toyota dealership and couldn't afford to rent an apartment. Blaine and I agreed that we would amicably live together on the boat until I was in a better position financially.

After a little over a year of painfully living together while mentally being separated, I finally got promoted to be the Customer Relations manager with a steady paycheck. A month later I moved off the boat into my own apartment. I gathered the couple of pieces of furniture that were ours that my sister was using. Then I started piecing together a new life on land by myself.

I had a bed and a kitchen table. I went back to my Mom's house to get the pottery kitchen items that I had kept. The rest of the apartment came together slowly. I was grateful that one of the salesmen I worked with let me use his credit at a furniture store so I could buy a couch, side table and chair with ottoman for my living area. It allowed me to pay him back in payments. It was extremely difficult to set up a new household by myself starting with very little, but I managed to do it. I finally got to a point where I felt settled in my new life.

Janet Charbonneau

Then the unimaginable happened. After almost a year in my new position, I was fired. I had been so excited to get my new position that I had agreed to have my position tied to the customer satisfaction surveys that the salesmen received from their customers. The salesmen were supposed to get me involved any time they had a dissatisfied customer. Unfortunately, I was not always involved and we ended up with a few months in a row of bad surveys. I was fired due to the rise of these bad surveys. I was devastated at losing my job. I had always excelled in all of my jobs, so I didn't even know how to react to my job loss.

Sitting in my small one-bedroom apartment, I searched for a new job. I truly felt lost. I didn't know where to go. I still sat in a huge puddle of debt. I was on unemployment which was unimaginable for me; I never thought in a million years that I would end up on unemployment! I could have moved back in with my Mom, but I didn't even have the money to rent a truck to move my stuff up there. Besides, I was too stubborn to give up!

I had been out of the technology world for more than eight years, so I could not easily fit back into it. I would have to learn new technology in order to get a job back in that field. Also, Charleston did not have a big technology sector. I had worked in the Research Triangle Park in North Carolina where there were a plethora of technology jobs, but down in Charleston, there were less than a handful available in the classifieds.

After living on a boat for a few years and having all of the blue-water sailing hours under my belt, I had studied for and achieved my Near Coastal 50-Ton Master Captain's license. I tried to find a job as staff on a large yacht, but I had no luck with that.

I looked for administrative assistant jobs because I felt that I had the skills for them, but they continued to elude me. I began going to networking events to meet business people in Charleston, hoping to find a job. Instead, the job found me. One day an idea popped into my head. Most of the people I had met at the networking events were busy business people and they had a hard time finding the time to get everyday chores done. When your job and life are too busy, it is hard to find time to go grocery shopping and clean the house. I started polling people at the networking events to see what types of everyday tasks that they had trouble completing on their own. I decided to open a personal assistance business to do all the things that others are too busy to do.

My business, Life a la Carte, was born. I had gathered several customers before I started the business, so I knew it would be successful. I cleaned houses, ran errands, catered parties, organized clutter, and paid customers' bills. The business steadily grew with referrals from my customers.

Even though I was getting new business coming in, I wasn't able to keep up with paying the credit cards that had been maxed out by my ex-brother-in-law. I managed to continue to pay two of them but had to quit paying the rest of them in order to be able to keep a roof over my head. My credit scores plummeted! I was devastated!

I ended up living from one job to the next. Some days I didn't know how I was going to pay the next bill, but then I would get another job just in time to pay it. It was frightening to be so alone and not know if you could pay your next bill. I felt like I was always on the brink of homelessness. I hated holidays because they interfered with my scheduled jobs and lost income for me. The lack of a secure steady paycheck was starting to weigh heavily on me.

I got to a point where I was able to hire a couple of people to work on some of the scheduled house cleanings for me, but after a year of that I was still barely paying my bills and the plethora of hours of work and after-hours paperwork were taking a toll on me. I was exhausted!

I had moved into a condo and had a roommate to be able to afford the lease. I had already lost one roommate when he had to move out of town quickly for a new job, leaving me scrambling to quickly find a replacement. Unfortunately, I was constantly worried about having that issue again. I also didn't have great luck with my roommates, so I spent most of my time in my bedroom.

I spent every weekday working on my business and every evening in my room. I couldn't afford to take a vacation or even afford to miss any days of work for fear of not being able to pay my bills. I felt so alone and afraid that there would come a day where I couldn't pay one of my bills. I knew I couldn't keep up this pathetic existence; I needed a change.

One of my friends owned an IT consulting business and had asked me previously to work for him. I didn't want to go back to that business since it had been so stressful in my last IT position, so I had turned down his suggestion. I was second guessing this decision and decided to meet with him to see what I could do to get back into that field. After meeting with him, I had a promise of a new job when his new contract came in. A couple months later I was back working in my Computer Science field.

I was very happy to finally have a steady income coming in again. I slowly started paying off my bills and getting into a stable life. After three years of working in my new job, I started feeling stagnant. I was supporting IBM software day in and day out and enjoyed my job, but had nothing outside of the job. I felt empty. I needed a goal to work towards. I yearned for something that I could be passionate about again.

I had been in an emotional rut for years. After being separated for over two years, we finally had gotten a divorce in 2010. Since then, I had not had any luck in the dating field. For the first few years, I was just emotionally unavailable. I was too guarded to attract anyone. While I thought I was open to a relationship, in reality, I really wasn't.

My recent dating history had consisted of a couple of short relationships but nothing that lasted or brought about anything close to the adventures I had with my ex-husband. I had been trying the online dating scene for several months, but that definitely was not working out. The only thing I was accomplishing with those dates

The Journey Inward

was gathering stories that had the possibility of becoming a hilarious "Fifty First Dates" saga for a future book.

I was about 75% done with writing a book about the motorcycle adventure but couldn't dredge up the discipline to actually finish it. I had fallen into a big black hole of boredom and felt stuck. Like a zombie, I was just going through my daily routine with no purpose.

After reflecting on the past ten years, I realized that I hadn't traveled in several years. I was yearning to explore a new place. The last few times I had traveled, I had my partner-in-crime, Blaine, along with me...and usually our two Golden Retrievers in tow. The last time I had traveled without Blaine was back in my 20s. I decided it was time to jump back on the horse (or motorcycle so to speak)...only this time completely on my own. What the hell was I thinking?

I believed that hiking the Camino would give me a challenge to help me prove that I could enjoy adventurous vacations on my own. I felt drawn to this hiking experience. I wasn't sure why I felt so driven to push myself to complete this pilgrimage, but I was. Most likely a mid-life crisis at 50. I decided that hiking the Camino de Santiago was an excellent idea for my 50th birthday!

We had been called crazy for both our sailing and our motorcycle adventures, so nobody was really surprised when I decided to take a few weeks off work to hike in northern Spain. There was one big difference between those adventures and this idea of walking 440 miles across northern Spain. I was doing this one alone, without a net, and I was petrified! I spent night after night convincing myself that I could do this. In fact, I had to do this!

Preparation

With less than three months before my birthday, I knew I needed to start preparing for this journey. I ordered my first two books about the Camino from Amazon. The first one was "Pilgrim Tips & Packing List Camino de Santiago: What you need to know beforehand, what you need to take, and what you can leave at home" by S. Yates. Since I had never been hiking before, I thought this would help me figure out what I needed for the trip. I had no clue where to start so this appeared to be a sensible beginning.

My second book was "A Pilgrim's Guide to the Camino de Santiago: St. Jean – Roncesvalles – Santiago" by John Brierley. It was a guidebook that broke the hike down to daily sections describing the route for each day, towns along the way, and the albergues and hostels in each town. The albergues (pronounced all-BEAR-gays) are pilgrim hostels usually consisting of numerous bunk beds within a room. Since the journey to Santiago is classified as a pilgrimage, the term "pilgrim", or the Spanish version, "Peregrino", is used for the people who hike the Camino.

In order to stay in the albergues, you must have a pilgrim's passport, known as a *credential*. The passport consists of a long, thick paper, folded like an accordion. It contains spaces for each albergue to place their stamp, or *sello*, proving your passage along the Camino. You can also receive stamps at churches and bars along the way. The term *bar* is used for the restaurants and cafés along the route. They serve alcohol at all times of the day when they are open, so the term *bar* is appropriate.

Shortly after starting to research the ins and outs of the Camino, I got a recommendation for one more guidebook, "Hiking the Camino de Santiago", by Anna Dintaman and David Landis. Like the guidebook by Brierley, it too listed the route for each day, towns along the way and albergues and hostels in each town, but it also listed amenities found in each town including bars, restaurants, supermarkets, ATMs, transportation, internet, medical services, and post offices. I felt like both guidebooks provided different information and perspectives, so I wanted to have both of them available for my hike.

The Camino is a large undertaking and a long journey. I wanted a way to capture my thoughts, share my experiences, and sort through my emotions. A journal was the perfect outlet and I found a website, trailjournals.com, already set up for hikers to log their journal entries. It was organized by different hiking destinations and the Camino de Santiago was one of them. I browsed through some of the Camino journals that already existed on this site and I became excited about my trip.

I felt giddy as I created my new Camino journal page where I could organize my journal entries so my family and friends could follow my journey. It was extremely easy to set up a new page. I figured out how to change my website URL from their generic URL to www.trailjournals.com/charbo to make it easier for me and others to remember. There was also a built-in counter that would keep track of the number of people that visited the page and a guestbook where anybody reading my journal could leave me a message. This adventure started to feel real as I wrote my first journal entry which described my plans in detail.

Janet Charbonneau

Journal Entry:

What Is This Journey?

What is this journey and why am I traveling to northern Spain to hike 440 miles? I will be hiking the Camino de Santiago. Wikipedia describes it as "The Camino de Santiago, also known by the English names Way of St. James, St. James's Way, St. James's Path, St. James's Trail, Route of Santiago de Compostela, and Road to Santiago, is the name of any of the pilgrimage routes (most commonly the Camino Francés or French route) to the shrine of the apostle St. James the Great in the Cathedral of Santiago de Compostela in Galicia in northwestern Spain, where tradition has it that the remains of the saint are buried. Many take up this route as a form of spiritual path or retreat for their spiritual growth." In a recent blog, I ran across this description of it: "The 800 kilometer El Camino dirt path is also known as the world's longest psychiatric highway." I like that description even better! They say there are three sections of the journey: the first third for the body (physical), the second third for the mind (mental) and the last third for the soul (spiritual). From all the journals and books that I have read, I believe that this progression from the body to mind to the soul is true and I am looking forward to that journey.

In 2014 there were over 200,000 people who walked the Camino along its many routes. Since it is considered a pilgrimage, those that walk these trails are called pilgrims. While there are many routes of the Camino, I will be taking the one called the French Way. It starts in St. Jean Pied de Port and runs 780 kilometers to Santiago de Compostela. I will be starting in Pamplona which is about three days into the recommended 33-day journey. I will fly to Madrid and take a train to Pamplona where I will begin my Camino adventure. I will be walking approximately 710 kilometers or 441 miles.

I will not be camping along the way or hauling a lot of food and cooking gear. If you have read the book or watched the movie Wild, it will not be quite as primitive. I will be staying in pilgrim hostels along the way. These hostels

The Journey Inward

are called albergues (pronounced al-BAIR-gays). For 5-10 Euros per night (5-11 US dollars), you can stay in one of these albergues. It may consist of a few beds in a room or 50 bunk beds in one room, so, yes, I will be bringing earplugs with me. Often both men and women sleep in the same room. I read one blog where the lady said that she slept with a different man every night along the way. Since she slept in mixed-gender rooms every night, I guess she did sleep with a different guy every night. Haha! The albergues usually provide a bed and a shower plus an area to hand wash and line dry your clothing. Sometimes a pilgrim meal is included which is a great source of camaraderie.

For meals, I plan to stop in the various towns and villages along the way. Because their cafés/restaurants don't open until later hours than Americans are accustomed to, the usual routine will be to get up and start walking early and then after a few miles stop to have breakfast. Most of these restaurants are called "bars" even though they are not bars in an American sense of the word. I imagine most of my meals will be at random stops along the way when my body needs a break and nourishment. It is also possible to buy a sandwich called a bocadilla which is a baguette-style bread with ham and cheese to take with you to eat for lunch along the way.

I am looking forward to meal times since this will be a wonderful time to get to know my fellow pilgrims. One of the best parts of the journey will be meeting all of the amazing people along the way. There is a possibility that I will be traveling with a friend of a friend, but even if traveling alone I will still not be alone. I will be meeting interesting people from around the world. I may walk with some of them or walk alone and meet up with them in future stops. These friendships are one of the things I miss most from my days when we cruised on our sailboat...meeting so many awesome people who are still friends to this day!

So why have I decided to take this journey? The first reason is that it has been on my bucket list ever since the first time I watched the movie "The Way" starring Martin Sheen. (If you haven't seen the movie, I highly recommend it. I believe it will give you a much better understanding of my trip.) The second reason is that I turn 50 this year in August and I wanted *to do something really special for my birthday. The third reason, which probably goes with the fact that I am turning 50, is for the growth of body, mind, and soul along the journey. Since there will be internet access along the way, I plan to update my journal daily or as often as I can. I hope this daily writing along with the journey will kick start my desire to finish my Hogs for Dogs book. I seem to have become lost lately in the "online dating from hell" path and want to find my way back to publishing this book which I believe is my purpose. I am hoping the Way of St. James will show me The Way.*

St. James the Great was the son of Zebedee and one of Jesus' twelve apostles. He is the Patron of Pilgrims and Laborers. St. James was a fisherman who became one of the first disciples to follow Jesus. Along with John and Peter, he was present during the raising of Jairus' daughter, the Transfiguration of Christ, and Jesus' Agony in the Garden Of Gethsemane. He is considered the first apostle to be martyred and his body was brought to Santiago de Compostela where he was buried. The pilgrimage to Santiago was well traveled in the Middle Ages but declined in the 16th century. In the 1980s the route became popular again with the modern-day pilgrim, attracting pilgrims from around the world.

I was wondering if I was crazy to even attempt this trip since I had never been hiking. I had no clue if I could even accomplish it. I had only three months before my birthday and I wasn't sure I was physically fit enough to hike that far, plus I had no hiking gear. One of my journal entries describes my search for the right hiking gear.

Journal Entry:

1st Time Hiker's Trek through the Forest of Hiking Gear

As the walking practice continues, I also wade through the unknown world of hiking gear! I have never hiked before…which means never owned hiking

The Journey Inward

boots, never owned a backpack, and never taken a long walk over five miles. How do you pick out hiking gear and accessories when you know nothing about hiking? You do lots of research and trial and error. My first pair of hiking boots was a pair that I picked out on my own at Dick's Sporting Goods. After less than 10 miles in them, I realized that they were giving me blisters and probably would continue to do so. Unfortunately, at that point, I had worn the boots and they couldn't be returned. For my next pair, I decided to make the three-hour trek to Greenville, SC to the closest REI and let the experts fit my next pair of boots for me. The best part of REI is that they have a one-year return policy...even if it has been worn but doesn't work for you. I spent three hours trying on boots and hiking sandals. I was grateful for the patience of the REI sales rep. I ended up with a great pair of boots that will be my hiking buddies on my Camino walk plus a pair of sandals that can be worn in the evenings and used for hiking if needed. My boots have already made it on a 9.5 and 13-mile trek through the city with me so far with no blisters.

When it came to backpacks, I was even more clueless!! Thank goodness for the experts at REI. I had read many recommendations about Osprey packs so when the backpack specialist at REI asked me what I was interested in I could at least mention that...perhaps sounding a little knowledgeable about backpacks...even though I was still clueless! He measured me and then fit me with an Osprey backpack while letting me know that they have a lifetime warranty...they will either fix it or replace it...for life. Had to love that! Sold on the brand...now how about the backpack? After fitting the backpack to me, my backpack expert added 15 pounds of weight in the pack and told me to walk around the store for 20 minutes. After feeling like a fool walking in a circle with a backpack on in the middle of the store, my backpack expert met up with me and asked me about the fit. It felt good and the weight was sitting properly on my hips and not on my shoulders. It was a go! I loved the backpack but hated the color. The only color in the store was Conifer Green which looked like a bright army green. Not my choice to live with for five weeks straight, so my backpack expert looked it up online and I fell in love with the Tarn Blue color. The store advertised a 25% discount which was not showing up online when I went to order, so I asked them to order it for me the next day and they managed to manually give me that 25% discount. I love REI!

Boots and backpack down...what else to figure out? Everything! There was so much more to decide. I purchased a 45-degree sleeping bag, but think I may return it for the 55 degrees one since I will be sleeping indoors, not in a tent. I spent a while looking for shirts that were quick drying shirts that also had a longer sleeve to protect my upper arm from rubbing against my body or backpack. Why are all the women's sleeves these little cap sleeves? And why do all the men's athletic shirts have high cut circular collars that look like they are going to choke me? After searching several outdoors stores, I finally found a great shirt by Calia, the Carrie Underwood collection. Loved the longer short sleeves and the look of the shirt as well as the quick dry, odor resistant qualities! I purchased the coral-colored one immediately and ordered another one in purple.

Another big decision was electronics. While many who walk the Camino recommend no electronics, I WILL NOT follow that recommendation. I agree that it is a pilgrimage and should be well spent experiencing the sights and sounds around you each day. But I have a history where I lost my Dad while I was in the Bahamas with limited communication and vowed I would NEVER do that again. We didn't have a satellite phone and they contacted the local police who were supposed to inform us on the morning check-in via VHF radio, but the word didn't get to me. I didn't find out my Dad was in the hospital for 36 hours and he passed away that night. My Mom is 89 and I unexpectedly lost a brother last summer, so I want to keep communication open with my family at all times. I made several decisions from that desire. I needed to upgrade my iPod so I ordered a new iPod Touch from Costco which allows me to carry my music with me as well as giving me the usage of iMessage for free texting using the Internet which is usually available in each town. This way I have easy communication with my sister who has an iPhone. Plus I decided to get a package on my Verizon phone to have a limited data/phone/text package for emergencies. I will also use my phone with the WhatsApp app to text for free with my Android friends. To assist with

The Journey Inward

keeping my two devices charged, I purchased a solar charger which I can attach to my backpack for daily recharging from the sun. I will keep my electronics off during my walking times to enjoy the scenery and sounds, but will definitely use them when I stop for the day to continue communication back home. It may be a pilgrimage, but I will not be isolated from my friends and family. I will continue to submit journal entries so they can be a part of this pilgrimage experience. I also decided to use my phone as my camera and purchased a new 64GB memory card to have one large enough to store the pictures that I will take on my journey. This provides a great multi-purpose use of my phone! Less weight is a good thing!!

I am four weeks away from leaving and I still have so many decisions to make! Rain poncho or rain jacket/pants? What about socks and liners? I'm still trying out different socks to find the best ones. What toiletries do I bring? No makeup but I am definitely taking deodorant which some suggest leaving behind to save weight in your backpack. I will carry the few extra ounces to smell decent!! I decided to carry walking sticks so I still need to select those. There are still so many decisions to make including what medical supplies to take, but I will definitely be carrying my doggy footprint duct tape with me to use over my "hot spots' to keep those blisters away!

I must have tried on every pair of boots in the store; the salesman was really nice and patient with me. In our conversations, he suggested using duct tape whenever I started to get a "hot spot" on my foot. The duct tape would become a barrier and prevent a full blister from forming. Before my hike, I found some purple-blue duct tape decorated with multi-colored dog prints. I purchased it and called it my Bailey tape since it reminded me of my Goldie, Bailey, who I lost in 2007.

Since I had shopped REI a great deal while preparing to move onto our sailboat, I was familiar with the store; what I didn't realize was that they had a one-year return policy. I wish I had known that before purchasing my first pair of boots in a store that wouldn't let me return them after wearing them. I was stuck with a $130 pair of boots that gave me blisters.

To make REI even better, they have a members rebate and they were able to look up my member info even though my last name had changed back to my maiden name and my address had changed several times since registering with them. It was actually kind of scary that I moved several times in different states and they were still able to track down my membership so easily with only the info on my driver's license!

After leaving REI, I drove around the surrounding area and found Cabela's, an outdoorsman store that I knew about since my brother had shopped those stores for many years for hunting and camping gear. I went in and looked around the entire store trying to get ideas of things I would need on my hike. After browsing the entire women's section and trying on several pairs of shorts, I found a great pair of cargo shorts by Columbia that was made of a quick dry material. I decided to purchase one pair and try them out. If they worked out, then I planned to purchase a second pair.

I had traveled to Greenville on my own so it was a very small step toward traveling alone again. I found a hotel that was close to both stores and was happy to see it was surrounded with lots of different stores and restaurants. I got used to eating by myself, but I did have company for dinner one night.

I had been chatting with a guy online who lived in Greenville and we decided to meet. So I combined my trip for camping gear with an online date. We met at a Japanese steakhouse where they cook everything in front of you. This was out of character for me. I usually only met for a drink on a first date to avoid suffering through a lengthy dinner if it ended up being a really bad date. Thankfully, we had a really good time during dinner and moved to another restaurant for after-dinner drinks.

At the end of the evening, I felt I had finally found someone worth a second date and he lived two hours away from me! This was

The Journey Inward

frustrating. I had been on numerous first dates in Charleston with no desire to go on a second date for various reasons and now I finally find someone worthy of a second date and he lived 2 hours away. Even though we both had a good time and were both attracted to each other, we decided the distance was too much to attempt future dates. This gave me hope that it was possible to find that someone special. Maybe the hike on the Camino would help me sort out my feelings on dating.

Upon returning from my first hiking gear shopping trip to Greenville, I realized how many items I still needed to purchase. I followed a Facebook group that dealt exclusively with questions about hiking the Camino. I posted my questions to the group and was grateful for the feedback from those who had already completed the hike. Wanting to learn more about the experience, I began to read many memoirs from others who had completed their Camino. I read *A Million Steps* by Kurt Koontz, *A Journey of Days* by Guy Thatcher and *The Way, My Way* by Bill Bennett. It was extremely helpful to read about the ups and downs on their journeys. I continued with my practice and preparations.

For a brief time, I thought my ex-husband, Blaine, was going to go on the trip as well. He is the one who introduced me to the movie, The Way, and he had wanted to hike the Camino for years. We have managed to still be best friends and it would have been fun to hike with him. He ended up not being able to go and I knew he was envious to see me hike it before he got a chance. Instead, he connected me with a friend from high school. Since Diane Bock also wanted to hike the Camino with Blaine, he connected the two of us via Facebook so we could explore the possibility of being travel buddies. Diane and I started chatting to get to know each other and the chats transitioned to discussions about hiking gear, training, and the numerous reservations to make the trip work.

We started discussing a starting point. I had four weeks of Personal Time Off that I planned to use, but I really wanted to start in

Pamplona. In the movie *The Way,* the characters stop at a set of pilgrim statues at the top of a mountain and I wanted to see those statues. They were just outside of Pamplona, so I decided to start there. I managed to get permission to work extra time before I left and take that comp-time for the extra week to be able to hike for five weeks. I was very grateful that both the owner of the company I worked for as well as the Project Lead for my project were both supportive of my hike.

Diane had originally planned to hike for four weeks, but when I set my timeframe for five weeks with definite dates, she decided to join me for the whole trip and meet me in Pamplona. I now had a hiking buddy!! I was thrilled to have someone hiking with me, especially since we seemed to have so much in common. We had never met; therefore, I hoped we would get along once we met in Pamplona.

Looking at the August/September timeframe for my hike, I researched the weather and the crowds on the Camino. The most popular months for pilgrims were June, July, and August, with August being the most popular month. Since August was also a very hot month, I ruled it out. That left September as my best option for fewer crowds and cooler weather.

It was mid-July and I had been preparing for the trip but had not made the commitment. I hadn't booked my flight yet. Diane and I had decided to fly out on August 29th, but the departure time was getting closer and I still did not have my flights booked. I had been looking at flights diligently for a couple of weeks. I knew how they were fluctuating in prices and I was ready to book when I saw a good price. I was ready to take the plunge. In my mind, purchasing this ticket took this trip from an idea to something real and tangible. I was finally making the commitment to go. So on July 17[th,] I purchased my tickets. There was no backing out now. I was going to Spain…whether my hiking buddy, Diane, went or not. I was excited to be going!

The Journey Inward

I contacted Diane and told her I had booked my flights. She had been researching her flights too. She was committed to going as well. We planned to meet in Pamplona. Since we had never met in person, we were taking a chance that we would get along fine. We were about the same age and were both in stagnant stages of life looking for a change.

She had been doing the online dating thing too, so she likened our meeting to a first date. "I feel like this is a very long first date....we will either get along very well or not talk to each other by the time it's over." That was so true! I was hoping we would get along and I would have a cool hiking buddy for my trip. However, I was also prepared to walk alone if we didn't get along. I didn't think that would be the case. My ex-husband knew both of us well and felt we would get along fine. Diane seemed like the perfect partner to join me on this journey.

After a month of having my boots and backpack, I needed to go back to REI and Cabela's for all the other stuff. I had less than a month before my August 29th departure date and I was running out of time. My best friend, Pam, heard that I was going and she thought it would be fun to join me in shopping. I was excited to have someone travel with me this time. On the morning of Saturday, August 8th, Pam, her little girl, Sara, and I made the trip back to Greenville.

Upon entering Greenville, we stopped at a restaurant I had enjoyed on my last visit. We wanted to eat lunch to fuel us for our shopping mission. With full stomachs, we left the restaurant and immediately headed to REI. I exchanged my sleeping bag for a lighter one rated for higher temps. I selected my first pair of walking sticks. Thankfully, the awesome REI salesman helped me figure out which ones would work best for me and gave me tips on how to use them.

Pam gave me feedback as I tried on numerous pairs of polarized sunglasses until we had narrowed it down to two pairs. I figured out which one would work better for my hike and purchased a protective, floral silk cover that doubled as a glass cleaner cloth. I found a medium dry sack that could be used for a couple different reasons. It could keep my phone, iPod, passport and other items dry if we encountered torrential rains or could keep my clothes dry while showering in tight shower facilities.

I wanted to purchase a wide-brimmed hat to protect my face and neck from the constant sun but had not found one I liked on my last shopping trip. As I tried on hats again, Pam critiqued each one with constructive feedback. I found one that we both liked and added it to the mound of items already in the cart. After debating for weeks on the decision of a rain jacket or poncho, I took the advice from many comments on the Camino Facebook group and selected a poncho that would fit over my backpack as I wore it. I selected a new fanny pack to wear in front of me and a silk money belt to wear under my clothes. This configuration would provide for easy retrieval of my phone and money and keep extra cash safe, separate from daily use cash. As my cart filled up, I threw in a small water-resistant notepad for daily notes as I walked and a camp towel. The list of needed items seemed to be endless. It was really fun to have Pam along on this trip to give me advice and feedback on everything!

As I looked at socks, one of the REI salespersons recommended Darn Tough socks. I was comparing those to other wool socks; therefore, I tried on both. The sales staff then researched the style hiking boot I had purchased, found my style and size in stock, and allowed me to test the socks wearing the same style boots that were at home in my closet. With a different sock on each foot and the hiking boots on, I climbed up and down on the fake rocks in the store. I felt pretty funny walking around in two different socks but it was a great way to compare them. I fell in love with the Darn Tough socks and they felt great alone with no sock liners! Plus they came in really fun colors and designs. I bought two pairs; one pair with purple, red, blue, and yellow stripes and a forest green pair that had a hot pink stripe along the top.

The Journey Inward

We went to Cabela's and I couldn't find the shorts that I had fallen in love with. I was upset with myself that I had waited so long to return for my next shopping trip and I had assumed the shorts would still be available. I decided to ask a saleswoman about them and she looked them up on her computer. They were available in their warehouse and she ordered another pair for me. I added a taupe colored pair to my wardrobe as that was the only color available in my size. I paid the extra shipping charge to have them shipped directly to me in Charleston. I hoped they would get to me in time for my trip since the estimated delivery date was only a few days before my departure.

As I examined every article of clothing in the women's section, I found a great thin and lightweight workout jacket to keep me warm. I continued shopping as my friend spent time showing her little girl the "dead zoo" (all the taxidermied animals that were on display). I wandered over occasionally for advice as I modeled the items I found.

We stopped by REI one last time on Sunday before we left Greenville so I could browse the clothes once more. We then ran by Mast General Store in downtown Greenville. In Mast General, I was able to find another shirt that would work well for hiking. I found a nice super lightweight white hiking shirt to use for sun protection and a great sarong/scarf that would serve many functions, such as a skirt if needed in churches.

I was now training almost daily, hiking outside when possible but primarily in the gym during a steamy Charleston summer. Here is the journal entry that explained one of my practice hiking trips.

Journal Entry:

Chicken Biscuit…the Path to Preparation and Practice

Chicken biscuit, chicken biscuit, chicken biscuit! How many of you have thought about that darn chicken biscuit for two hours? I did last Saturday

Janet Charbonneau

as I was walking the 6.5 miles to Bojangles. While I am not usually food motivated and rarely eat fast food, I was on a mission that day! Walk to Bojangles and back with my hiking boots and backpack making it a 13-mile hike. Three and a half miles further than I had been previously and carrying a backpack for the first time...which ended up weighing 8.5 pounds (a bit more than I had planned on). While it wasn't a very scenic route, it was a well-known area and I had a friend checking in with me to make sure I was doing well. I had my backup ride if needed!

At 6:15 in the morning, I set out in 76-degree weather with 97% humidity. While it was not hot yet, the humidity made it hard to breathe! The first two miles of the route were on the nicely shaded greenway, but the majority of the route was on a sidewalk next to a four-lane road with not a whole lot to see. Thus, the infatuation with the chicken biscuit to keep me motivated since the scenery certainly did not. The last 2 ½ miles to Bojangles consisted mainly of trees with nothing else in sight. It was a long, boring, straight stretch and I kept looking for the stoplight marking the turn to my last half mile...where was that darn stoplight? Finally, I saw the light and turned for my last half mile which was my most difficult stretch with no sidewalk and very little grass to walk on. So I walked on the road and hopped to the side when cars passed by. They probably thought I was crazy! I made really good time on the way to Bojangles and was finally able to sink my teeth into a nice, hot, juicy chicken biscuit! YUM!

The route back was not as easy; maybe because I didn't have that same incentive to walk. At 9:00 a.m. the temperature was already into the 80s and the sun was overhead so I did not have as much shade. I stopped often to drink the unsweetened tea that I had put into my sports bottle at Bojangles along with lots of ice that was melting quickly. After my 11th mile, I stopped at the BiLo grocery store for a Gatorade and my friend stopped to visit with me on my much-needed break. Thankfully, they had a couple of tables near the deli area where we were able to sit and chat.

The last two miles were tough. The duct tape which had protected my right ankle for 11 miles was cutting into my ankle after my break so I limped into a shady spot to re-tape my ankle. After a few minutes walking it felt

The Journey Inward

back to normal and I made it home. It took me 5 ½ hours to walk the 13 miles with two breaks which is very close to a normal day on the Camino...averaging about 15 miles per day. Mission accomplished! I was thrilled that I had just hiked the distance equivalent to an average day on the Camino. I was more confident that I could achieve my goal.

My previous longest trek had been a 9 ½ mile walk up to Subway and back...yes, again, a food- motivated walk. I left at 7:00 a.m. and it was brutally hot on my way back from that hike. Even though it was in the mid-80s, I had almost no shade and the heat indexes were in the 90s. Again that day I stopped at BiLo for a Gatorade and as I walked home my legs got extremely tired. My latest hike to Bojangles was a big improvement over this one.

I've had to leave early in the mornings in order to be done by late morning since I am practicing in hot and humid Charleston, SC....in the summer. I believe the early morning departures will be similar to my Camino experience. I will be leaving early in the morning to walk in the cooler hours and to make sure I get to the albergues early enough to get a bed for the night. I think it will become a food motivated journey again as I look forward to stopping for the meal and the break....as well as the glass of red wine at the end of walking for the day.

My practicing has also consisted of many days and evenings at the gym with my hiking boots and backpack along with me on the treadmill whenever the Charleston weather is too hot for outside practice. I put a sign on my backpack that says "Training to hike the Camino de Santiago in Spain" so the people at the gym don't think I am crazy for being on a treadmill in hiking boots carrying a backpack! I have started to use the incline on the treadmill to practice the inclines on my upcoming journey and those inclines have kicked my butt! I will need to practice with more inclines and will also walk Charleston's famous Ravenel bridge which is the only thing in Charleston with an incline. Another area of practice is walking on the beach barefoot to toughen up my still-tender feet.

After all this walking practice I realized that I need to take some days off from walking and work on the weight machines to keep all of my other *muscles in shape! My walking plan is to work on increasing distances with heavier backpacks until I can walk the 15 miles with a 15-pound backpack. While I continue to prepare for my long journey, soon the day will be here and I will embark on my long walk through Spain whether I am ready or not! As those who have walked it before me have said, the Camino will provide and I believe that I will somehow manage those 15 mile days to be able to accomplish that hike from Pamplona to Santiago!*

I had promised my Mom that before I went hiking I would get a physical. I hadn't had one in years and thought it was a good idea to make sure I was healthy before beginning this long, strenuous hike. Crossing my fingers for a good outcome, I went to a local Doctor's Care and got my physical. When the nurse practitioner came in to give me the results of my EKG, she said it was so pretty that she wanted to hang it on her refrigerator. My Mom had been told by her doctors that she has a healthy heart, so maybe I inherited that from my Mom. I was happy to hear that my heart was in good shape! Everything else came back fine so I was good to go from the health aspect. It had been a while since I had gotten a tetanus shot so I opted to get that as a precaution. No other shots were recommended and I was done after one shot. I was extremely grateful that I was told that I was healthy and was given the green light to proceed with my hike.

A few years earlier I had problems with my right knee, but I started taking chia seeds every day and they had eliminated the joint pain. With all of my practicing, my knees were still feeling good, but I decided that I would take a knee brace just in case. I would also take my Triple-Flex pills with glucosamine, chondroitin, and MSM to hopefully keep the knees from aching. I wanted to bring the chia seeds instead, but really didn't know what I was going to have available to mix them in, so I opted for the Triple-Flex.

As I got closer to my travel date, I started gathering all of my stuff for my hike. I thought the sleeping bag was going to be too heavy so I ordered a silk sleep sack from Amazon and found a small very

The Journey Inward

lightweight fleece blanket that would roll and compress into a very small sack. These combined were much lighter than the sleeping bag. I also ordered an adapter for charging my electronics and a tripod case for my trekking poles. I had heard that many times you could not bring them on the plane and that they had to be checked. Putting them into a tripod case also enabled me to check in the other items I couldn't carry on, like scissors.

The Camino Pilgrimage dates back over a thousand years and, as you might expect, comes with a variety of tradition. One tradition is to attach a scalloped shell to your backpack. There are many interpretations of the symbolism of the scalloped shell and one of them is that the lines of the shell represent the many roads that converge into one point, Santiago.

I wanted to have a shell before I left. I looked online and found a place to order the shells. I ordered four of them to have a choice and a couple of spares to work with. When they arrived, I asked a coworker to drill two holes in each one. I told him there were extras, so he could practice with the first one, if necessary. He did an excellent job. He brought all four of them back with two precise holes in each one of them. I contacted Diane to see if she had a shell yet and she did not so I told her I would bring one for her.

A few weeks before I was leaving, I stopped by my bank to order Euros so that I would have local currency when I arrived in Spain. The majority of cafes, bars, restaurants, alburgues, and hostels operated on a cash basis only, so I wanted to arrive prepared. I ordered 200 Euros to get started; the guidebooks said that there were ATMs along the way where you could withdraw more Euros. My banker put a note in my file stating that I would be out of the country for five weeks, so nothing would happen to my account when they started to see overseas withdrawals.

For budgeting, I had read the recommendations in the guidebook, Hiking the Camino de Santiago. It stated "On a strict budget, you may be able to walk the Camino for as little as 15 Euros per day if you stay in the cheapest albergues, cook your own meals, hand wash your clothing and forego any luxuries. A more comfortable daily budget of 30 Euros gives you the freedom to eat in restaurants, upgrade to more comfortable albergues, have the occasional coffee or glass of wine in a café, use a washing machine periodically and pay entrance fees to museums. With 50 Euros or more a day, you could upgrade to modest private accommodations, eat more adventurous restaurant meals and treat yourself to a few other luxuries."

I decided on a budget of 30-35 Euros per day for planning purposes. I also knew that if we decided to get more private accommodations, then I would go over that budget and I was fine with that plan. Therefore, the 200 Euros would cover the first few days of the trip. I really didn't want to travel with more than 200 Euros at a time. A couple of days before my departure date, I went back to the bank to pick up my Euros.

The day before my departure, I really started to panic. While I had been nervous about my trip for some time, it had been getting worse the closer I got to my departure date. I realized that I was petrified to go over there. I would have given anything at that time to simply cancel all my plans. I was nauseous from the fear of this unknown trip. I didn't feel prepared and was scared to travel by myself to Spain. I had never traveled overseas by myself and it had been over 20 years since I had traveled without a partner. I was hoping that I would hit it off with my new travel buddy so we could conquer the Camino together…two single women not letting anything stop us!

The Journey Inward

The Adventure Begins

On the day of departure, I got a text from Diane that her flight had been changed at the last minute. This meant that I was going to have to navigate the bus system in Madrid to the train station alone as well as navigate the train station and train change in Zaragoza. When I arrived in Pamplona, I would have to walk to the hotel alone in a strange foreign city where I didn't know the language. As I read the text, I sat down and the fear swept over me. I had felt more comfortable knowing that I would have Diane there to figure things out together and now I was going to have to make it through the bus station, train station and a walk to the hotel in a foreign city all by myself. I had to force myself to keep moving to overcome the fear gripping me and get to Pamplona on my own to meet Diane.

Even though I was only a few hours away from leaving, I still did not know how much my backpack weighed. After packing everything in my backpack, I went to the gym to weigh it. It weighed around 20 pounds. I went home to determine what I could leave behind. There wasn't much I was willing to give up, but I took a couple of items out and decided I could leave things behind along the way as I found that I would not need them. I was bringing two guidebooks and I planned to leave one of them at the first albergue. Diane and I had agreed that I would bring "A Village to Village Guide to Hiking the Camino De Santiago: Camino Frances:

Janet Charbonneau

St Jean - Santiago - Finisterre" byAnna Dintaman and Diane would bring "A Pilgrim's Guide to the Camino de Santiago: St. Jean • Roncesvalles • Santiago" by John Brierley. Just in case something happened and we didn't walk together, I wanted to bring my copy of Brierley's guide and would leave it at the first albergue if we did walk together. I also would leave an extra power adapter once I verified my other adapter worked fine. After reviewing every item again, I repacked everything into my backpack and nervously paced as I waited for my friend, Pam, to pick me up.

I was ready to leave but I knew I had another hour before Pam would pick me up. The hour felt like 4 hours; it dragged on as I paced. I had a huge lump in my throat and a gnawing feeling deep down in the pit of my stomach. I was extremely nervous but also tremendously excited to start this adventure. Finally, I saw her car pull up and I knew this was the point of no return.

As she dropped me off at the airport, Pam sensed my nervousness and offered me the encouragement that I needed to not run and hide. I swallowed hard and tried to keep my composure as I said my farewells to her. I really just wanted to break down into tears and tell her how scared I was, but I refrained. I pulled out every ounce of strength I had and moved on to the start of my new experiences. Little did I know this was just the start of the lessons that the Camino would teach me about my own strength. She took the "here I am, heading to my new adventure" pictures and told me she would be following me along the way. I needed to hear that!

I flew out at 5:00 p.m. from Charleston, SC to Atlanta and thankfully had plenty of time to catch my connecting flight. My nerves continued to haunt me as I navigated the connecting flight knowing what lay before me in Spain. As I settled into the nine-hour flight, the flight attendants served a pre-dinner drink. I asked if they had any bourbon and she said they had Woodford Reserve which is a more upscale bourbon than I usually drink and it was included in the

The Journey Inward

flight! Sweet! I ordered a Woodford Reserve on the rocks and began to relax.

I was happy I had a tiny person beside me, thus had plenty of room in my seat. Dinner was pretty tasty for an in-flight meal and they served a delicious red wine with it. I was surprised the wine was so good. It paired well with the triple chocolate brownie for dessert. The flight seemed to go by quickly since they kept serving good food and drinks most of the time!

After the relaxing flight to Madrid, I arrived 30 minutes early. It was only 9:20 in the morning and my train did not leave until 12:30. Thankfully the signs in the airport were in English as well! I retrieved my checked bag with my hiking poles, pocket knife, and other liquid items and went to look for a bus. After wandering outside not knowing what the heck I was looking for, I went back inside to ask at the Information booth. Thankfully the lady at the information booth spoke English and was able to direct me to the area for the buses to the train station. After finding the correct bus, I made it to the train station with plenty of time to spare. I went to the Renfe checkout stations to have them explain my ticket. The attendant showed me I was in coach 3 and my seat assignment. "Coach 3" was which car of the train your seat was in. It was very helpful to learn that piece of info! At least I knew where to go on the train.

Having an hour to wait for the train, I went to find a restroom. I found one with several stalls and no toilet paper in any of them. Thankfully I had come fully prepared. It had been suggested to bring a travel roll of toilet paper during the hike in case a pit stop was needed between towns. I laughed since I expected to use it during my hike, but not at the train station! Next, I found a comfortable seat and attempted to use the internet. I was unsuccessful after several frustrating attempts to connect to their wifi. I finally gave up and decided to watch the various other passengers as they arrived at the station.

Once on board, I easily found my seat. I was surprised that it wasn't very crowded. It was very comfortable so I closed my eyes and rested for a while as we sped on to Zaragoza. After I got off the train at the Zaragoza station, I looked around for some clue on how to get to the next train. I kept finding exits out of the train station, but no directions on how to get to my next train. Frustrated, I finally found someone who worked at the station but she spoke no English. I showed her my ticket and she pointed me in the right direction. Once I walked up the staircase, I finally found the area to wait for my next train. A wave of relief washed over me as I knew this was the last hurdle to get to Pamplona, my starting city of the Camino.

When I arrived in Pamplona, I knew I was within walking distance of the hotel but only had a high-level map to follow. The butterflies were back in my stomach. I headed out in what I believed to be the right direction but could not find any street signs to be sure. I was getting pretty nervous...lost in a foreign country.

After walking a bit more I asked a gentleman who spoke no English. I showed him my map and he pointed me in the right direction and motioned up, up, up. I started up a hill and continued on. I stopped at one point and looked around, but my route was still going up so I continued on. There was a river to my left side which was showing on the map, so I believed I was still going in the right direction.

I kept looking for street signs but didn't see any. How could they have no street signs? Maybe they were there and I just didn't know what I was looking for. I continued walking up as he had said, as I trusted his up, up, up directions. Finally, I ran across one of the Camino symbols! It was a blue sign with a yellow symbol representing the scalloped shell. I was overjoyed to see it. It was my first time seeing this symbol in person which would guide me the entire distance to Santiago. A huge wave of relief flowed over me. I now knew the way! My guidebook could get me from here. Thank goodness for great directions!

The Journey Inward

I got out my guidebook and followed it to the correct street. I wandered up and down this short street to find the hotel. I didn't see the hotel sign and again felt my panic rising. How could it not be right here? The street name was Calle Comedias and I was starting to feel that I was in a strange comedy where the joke was on me. I meticulously followed the numbers on the doors until I was in front of the hotel. The doors were set a few feet back from the rest of the building and I finally saw the hotel sign above the doors in a little alcove. I let out a sigh of relief and felt the tension flow out of me; one more hurdle crossed. I had managed to navigate via buses, trains and walking in this foreign country, not being able to speak Spanish. My first Camino lesson…I can survive on my own.

Since the reservation was in Diane's name, I decided to wander around the corner to the Plaza del Castillo which advertised having wifi (pronounced *weefee*). I found a bench where I could finally relax. I took a picture of the plaza and uploaded it to Facebook, so my family and friends would know that I had made it there safely. I noticed that my Facebook post containing my departure picture from the airport had 104 likes and around 20 people commenting. I appreciated the support from afar!

After about an hour I still hadn't heard from Diane and was getting tired of hanging out in the plaza. Not knowing when Diane would arrive I went to the hotel to see if I could wait in their lobby. To my amazement, they let me into the room before Diane arrived, even with the reservation in her name. And they didn't even make me pay anything up front. They said I could wait for Diane to arrive and pay at that time. After another hour went by and I still hadn't heard from Diane, I felt guilty being in a room that wasn't paid for. I went back down to the reception desk and asked if I could pay half the bill. They let me pay half and Diane could pay the remaining half when she arrived.

I went back upstairs to my room and relaxed on the balcony overlooking the narrow, brick street. It was a beautiful view with all the shops and restaurants below. While there was no space in between, it appeared that each street address was a different building with varying colors and textures (different bricks or concrete). Even all the balcony structures were different.

I noticed that my Garmin Vivofit was showing the incorrect time. It was still on Eastern Daylight Time and I wanted it to show the current time in Spain. I googled the answer and figured out how to change the time by synchronizing it to my phone. This was how I was going to track my steps per day. I wanted it to have the correct time zone for accurate step counts.

I continued to pace from the room to the balcony. I wanted a shower but didn't want to miss any communication with Diane. I was also becoming extremely hungry as I hadn't eaten anything since the last meal on the plane early that morning. I wanted to wait for Diane so we could eat dinner together. I regretted not grabbing a snack at the train station when I had arrived in Pamplona.

As I was standing on the balcony, I suddenly heard the door open and finally got to meet Diane! She was around 5'8" with an athletic figure. Her face was framed in long, wavy blond hair and she flashed a friendly, pearly white smile. We immediately started catching up with our adventures that day and I learned that Diane's tripod case did not make it to Madrid. Therefore, she didn't have her trekking poles and most of her toiletries! She would have to make plans for delivery somewhere along our hiking route, a difficulty given the fact we would be moving every day.

We both took showers and changed out of our travel clothes. We were very hungry and ready to find some dinner. We walked around the entire square where I sat earlier looking for wifi. We found a nice outdoor café for dinner. I had to laugh at the café. The sign overhead said English spoken here and none of the servers seemed to speak English! Haha! We ordered dinner by pointing to our menu items. I ordered nachos and ended up with a huge plate of nachos that had barbecue sauce on it. Weirdest nachos ever! I ate until I was full,

The Journey Inward

tending to eat around the barbecue sauce areas and the plate was still full when I was done. It was huge! After dinner, we wandered the streets and then stopped at an outdoor bar for a drink. I had to love Spain so far... $2 beers with dinner and $2 wine at the bar!

Back at the hotel, we got our packs ready for the hike. I had brought the scalloped shells for both of us to attach to our packs. We used the string that I had brought with me and figured out how to attach them to our backpacks. We unpacked and repacked our backpacks trying to get the most frequently used items on the top.

As I lay in bed, I knew I would have a hard time falling asleep. Not only was there a loud raucous crowd partying in the narrow streets below our room, but tomorrow would be the first day of a long journey. We would be venturing out into the unknown. One thing that kept me excited for tomorrow's adventure was that we would get to visit Alto de Perdon where the pilgrim statues resided! That is the main reason that I chose Pamplona as a starting point. If nothing else, we would be fulfilling one of my goals tomorrow.

Janet Charbonneau

Pamplona to Muruzabal

Day 1 of 31 (August 31st):
Kilometers: 19.7
Miles: 12.3

We woke up tired from the travel day but excited to start our hike. Day one was finally here! We had no idea what adventures lay ahead of us. Were we ready? Did we have everything we needed? How many miles was this journey again? 441? Really? Why had I convinced myself that I could hike this far with no previous hiking experience?

I climbed out of bed and mentally prepared myself for this journey. As I only had two hiking outfits it wasn't hard to decide what to wear since I had traveled in my other outfit the previous day. I brushed my teeth and combed through my hair the best that I could. I had no curling iron to curl my bangs, so I did the best I could with them. There was no makeup to put on, so getting ready was fairly quick.

As I packed my recently used items, I again reorganized my backpack as I reassessed those items that I thought I would need to access during my daily hike. I finally gave up and figured that after a couple of days on the road I would eventually come up with an appropriate packing scheme.

When we went to check out, we realized that we could probably get our pilgrims' passports stamped. We asked if they had one and we got our first stamp on the Camino! It was in blue ink and it said Hostales Pamplona with their phone number and address...very plain, but it was our first stamp and it showed our starting point. How exciting!

As we turned to leave, we were greeted with the Camino greeting, "Buen Camino." It is a greeting we would hear and use often. It translates to "Good Way" in English. It is a greeting that is given to a pilgrim to wish them well on their way. We would hear it from other pilgrims as well as from the locals as we walked by. We used it often to wish our fellow pilgrims well.

With a deep breath and a smile, I turned towards the door, ready to embark into the unknown. As we left our hotel I had to quote Martin Sheen in The Way and say "Here we go!" Thankfully I had crossed the Camino path the day before and I knew how to get us back to that part of the path. The path through Pamplona was marked on the sidewalks by circular silver discs with the Camino shell symbol on them. As long as we continued to see those discs, we knew we were headed in the right direction. This was comforting as we navigated our way out of Pamplona.

The buildings of the city gave way to a lone road and the first part of the walk seemed pretty tame. I assessed my equipment as I walked; my boots were comfortable and my backpack was sitting pleasantly on my hips. I felt that I had done a good job with those two selections.

Now that we had navigated out of the city and were following the only road out there, Diane and I began to chat. She had known Blaine from high school, but she asked me where I had met him and how long we had been married. I told her that I had actually met him when we were both on the booster club for our minor league hockey team. We were married for fifteen years; the last three of those years we had been separated. It had been five years since our divorce. She asked me why we divorced. Even though the details were very personal and painful, I opened up to her and told her what had happened. I figured if we were going to spend the next 30 days hiking with each other, then it was good to be open to her. Maybe we could learn things from each other.

After hearing the details, she asked about our current friendship. She said we seemed to still be good friends. I told her that we were. We had gone for a few years where we really didn't talk much to each other. I wasn't crazy about the relationship he was in at the time, so we kind of drifted apart, talking every few months. He had moved to Florida, so I think the extra distance also contributed to that. I think I needed the space to work on learning to be single again. But, to be honest, it was also a time that I withdrew a lot from everybody. After a few years, our communication became more frequent. Since we both knew each other so well, we started chatting more often when we needed some advice. Knowing the other person so well, we were able to give each other a different perspective to help resolve the problem. Therefore, we had become close friends again.

Diane told me about her divorce. During her separation, her husband would reel her in whenever he wanted or needed something, then he'd passive aggressively make her feel inadequate. This was one of the things that she needed to release during her Camino. She told me about her two daughters. The oldest was 22 and in nursing school. Her youngest was 21 and in her last year of college. They had been really supportive of her quest to hike the Camino. Her Mom asked her why she was making that hike and her response was, "because I can." I told her that my family was used to my crazy adventures so they hadn't really questioned me about why I wanted to go. They just wanted me to keep in touch so that they knew I was safe every day.

The conversation migrated to our jobs. We were both very grateful that we were able to take five weeks off of our jobs to be able to hike the Camino. She told me about her job as a Clinical Research Administrator at the University of Wisconsin-Madison. I then shared my job as an IT consultant, supporting IBM applications on a software integration project.

The Journey Inward

We walked 5.7 kilometers to our first stop in Cizor Menor. We found a café and were too thirsty for coffee so we each had a Coca-cola zero (pronounced *thero*) with a croissant. It was only three Euros (around $3.50 USD) for both. My croissant was chocolate. It was yummy and very decadent for me since I never ate pastries! It was a delicious breakfast for the first one on our journey!

We headed back out and started our long rocky walk up to the pilgrim statues. It was 8.4 kilometers of very rocky and steep climbing! Since I had trained in the Lowcountry of Charleston, SC I was not prepared for this ascent! Diane had trained climbing mountains and was used to it. She was also taller with long legs so she just trotted on up and I lagged behind huffing and puffing...and huffing and puffing.

We stopped in Zariquegui for a drink and I was very thankful for the break! Diane bought some excellent watermelon which was refreshing! I was introduced to the sports drink called Aquarius. It is like Gatorade that we have back in the United States. It was recommended by a friend I knew from high school and it was quite thirst-quenching! He recommended the white version which was a nice lemon citrus flavor. It was my new favorite thirst-quenching drink in Spain! The café had a couple of lime green tables with aqua umbrellas outside, so we sat down for a rest.

As we walked, I received a message from back home that one of my favorite motivational authors/speakers, Wayne Dyer, had passed away. I owned many books by him and had gotten a chance to listen to him speak twice at Hay House conferences. He even autographed one of my books. His teachings were key in helping me get through a very tough time in my life. I was extremely saddened to learn of his passing, but it was a reminder to use what I had learned from him while hiking the Camino. It was very symbolic that he passed away as I started my Camino. I felt he was on the path with me, cheering me on.

We continued with the grueling ascent. I was starting to feel like a fat little tub trying to climb up the mountain under my large pack as

Diane quickly shimmied up the path in front of me. I would stop every once in a while and turn around to see where we had come from and to enjoy the nice view. This climb up the hill also set the precedence of our daily hikes. While we started out together, Diane and I eventually would split up for most of our daily walks, which gave us both the time for personal reflection which I believed was an important part of the Camino.

Each time I turned around I could see the large city of Pamplona in the background with brown fields surrounding the winding, rocky beige path we were following up the mountain. It would give me a chance to catch my breath. I kept thinking about the pilgrim statues at the top of this mountain for motivation. Even after all of my training, I felt really out of shape!

We finally made it up to the top of the rocky climb. As we reached Alto de Perdon, we were greeted by the pilgrim statues! So cool! They were bronze-colored, wrought iron silhouettes of pilgrims with their heads bent into the wind. Some were on horses, while some of them walked. Some were children and some were adults. A dog was walking alongside them. There were around 10 statues in all. The inscription on one of the statues says "Donde se cruza el Camino del viento con el de las estrellas" which means "Where the way of the wind crosses the way of the stars". It was extremely windy up there, so the statue's wording seemed very appropriate.

We could also see dozens of wind turbines stretched out for miles on the mountains surrounding us. Each wind turbine was tall and white with three blades turning in the wind. It was such a beautiful sight! It was wonderful to see that they used wind power here for electricity.

We chatted with another group of pilgrims and Diane took a picture of their group in front of the statues for them. They seemed like a really fun group! There was a refreshment cart attached to a Jeep-like vehicle parked near the pilgrim statues which was a good idea after that climb. Since we had recently stopped for our drink in the last town, we just took our pictures of the pilgrim statues and moved on.

Being on the top of the mountain, we turned to look at the trail ahead. We saw the beige, rocky trail disappear into a group of scrub brush and trees and later appear beyond the trees at the bottom of the mountain. It then zigzagged back and forth up hills, around trees, and ended up in a small town far off in the distance. Having satisfied ourselves with the visit at the pilgrim statues and eager to get to our albergue, we started back on the trail.

While descending the mountain, we ran across an Italian guy riding his bike up the mountain headed in the opposite direction. He stopped in front of us which we found quite odd and then he looked at Diane and kept saying, "Limoncello". He kept using his hands and speaking in Italian, but she had no idea what he was trying to tell her. She looked to me for help, but I had no clue what he was trying to say either. He was very animated! Frustrated that we didn't understand him, he finally leaned over his bike and started rearranging her backpack as she looked at him in disbelief! He was trying to tell her that she was carrying it too low. He pulled it up and gave her directions to tighten certain areas. I was standing behind her and laughing at his antics. Diane said it actually felt much better...even after that manhandling from the Italian guy! And now Diane had a new nickname, "Limoncello." When he was done, he went along his way and we continued on as we laughed about what had just occurred.

Our descent was not much easier than the climb up the mountain. It was extremely rocky and tough on my knees. During our climb down we were met by the granddaughter of one of the owners of the albergue in the town Muruzabal. It was very brave of her to walk that rocky climb to hand out flyers for her family's albergue, Albergue El Jardin de Muruzabal. It looked very nice so we decided to stay there and we were extremely happy that we did. They had some private rooms so we selected one of their private rooms that shared a bath with another room.

It was 20 Euros per person for our private room, but it included breakfast and we weren't quite ready to be thrown into a room with lots of other people on our first night out. We decided it was worth the extra money. As we paid, we got our first albergue stamp in our passport. It was in black ink with the albergue name in a half circle with plants inside it. It was then dated and it appeared odd to me until I realized that they put the day of the month first, followed by the month and then the year.

We walked around the albergue and went outside near the pool. It looked very inviting, but it began raining so we went back inside. After about 10 minutes of settling down in our room, the bottom fell out of the sky and it poured with the wind howling. It looked like a hurricane blowing through! I cannot even imagine being out in that weather! We were very grateful that we had decided to stop early. We were starting to learn to listen to what the Camino was telling us and that we could change our minds on where we would stay each night.

Our Camino routine began as we took showers, changed into evening clothes, washed our clothes from the day, and then went to get a drink and relax. I was used to drying my hair with a hair dryer after washing it since it was so thick and took forever to dry. That was a luxury I was learning to do without. Instead, I had to just brush it out and tousle it a little to try to get a little curl. Since I had done this a lot when living on the sailboat, I had to again get used to a more natural me.

They had a washer and dryer, so we used them to wash and dry our clothes for the day along with the clothes that we had traveled in the day before. I was happy to have a set of evening clothes so I could wash both pairs of hiking clothes at the same time. The rain had subsided, so as our clothes were washing, we grabbed our drinks and headed out onto the covered front porch to sit at the long table.

That evening we had an awesome pilgrim's dinner that started with a salad topped with tomatoes, onion, egg, and tuna. It was accompanied by wonderful bread and, of course, red wine. The next course included pasta, roasted red peppers, and tortilla Espanola (a tasty egg and potato dish). We finished off with some ice cream. All of that food and drink for only 11 Euros! Sweet! The meal was prepared by the young girl we met on the trail and her mother. The father and grandfather served the meal. Our first pilgrim's dinner was fantastic!

We ate with a girl from San Francisco, a girl from Germany, a couple from Denmark, a girl from Norway and a guy who didn't speak English so no clue where he was from. It was really fun to chat with everyone to see where they were from and to hear their wonderful stories. This was definitely going to be the best part of the Camino…the people! It was truly a memorable evening!

Steps: 21,354

Janet Charbonneau

Muruzabal – Villatuerta

Day 2 of 31 (September 1st):
Kilometers: 22.2
Miles: 13.8

We began our day with breakfast at the albergue which was included in the price of the room. There was cereal, bread, fruit, and yogurt along with coffee and juices. It was nice to be able to sit and eat breakfast before heading out on our second day on the Camino.

Due to the crazy rain and winds the previous day, we spent the day sloshing through the mud! We passed a church in Obanos with stained glass windows with the Camino symbol of a scalloped shell in them. As we were coming out of Obanos we saw a beautiful rainbow which was promising after our wild thunderstorm the previous day.

After a short walk, we entered Puerta la Reina. As we were exiting, the trail pointed one way but there were marks/words that made it look like the other way was correct so we stood there and debated. We saw an older local couple probably in their 70s and Diane went to ask the gentleman which way to go. He was a little shorter than Diane and wore blue jeans rolled up on the bottom and a yellow button-down shirt. He pointed her to the correct way and then proceeded to tell her the rest of the directions for our day...all in Spanish!

Diane had no clue what he was saying although she did hear the word "montaña" several times! It was so funny to watch him explain to her what the rest of the day would include with his arms gesturing wildly, while she nodded her head, not understanding any of his directions.

He spent about 10 minutes talking to her and all we got out of it was to stay straight and not take the left turn that had confused us. We laughed as she joined me again, both of us recognizing the humor of his explanation in Spanish. We knew we had taken the correct path when we finally crossed the arched bridge leading out of town.

We would get used to having to make decisions once in a while when arrows were pointing in two different directions. Sometimes the other set was directing you to a nearby albergue instead of the Camino route. The route was marked by a mixture of official markers and spray painted yellow arrows. If the arrows were painted in white, then they were leading to something else and not the Camino route. The yellow arrows were painted on everything: streets, rocks, signs, buildings, wood stakes, etc., so you had to stay aware of your surroundings to make sure you saw the yellow arrows. Sometimes, they were large and you couldn't miss them. Other times they were small, so awareness was key.

Our day consisted of hard, steep, rocky climbs. We wandered up and up on a brick-paved pathway through one of the little towns. At the top of the hill, we stopped at a little market for a snack. Many of the towns in this region were literally built into the hills and the cobblestone streets were, according to Diane, "like walking the hills of West Virginia".

I purchased a peach and Diane bought some meat and cheese. We found a step to sit on and enjoyed our snack while we chatted. It was a relaxing break.

As we sat, I confided in Diane that our discussion yesterday about my divorce made me think harder about it. While I thought I had finally accepted the divorce and was at peace with Blaine and me still being friends, I realized that I was still holding resentments inside me. My resentments were all based on finances. I hated the financial situation that I had been in since the failed business. My credit score was hideous since I had to stop paying the credit cards after I lost my job.

I resented the fact that I had sold my BMW to purchase the fifth wheel RV that we lived in while working on the business in Mississippi. Blaine had purchased that BMW Z3 for me the year before we sold our house and went cruising. I had decided to keep it when we went cruising. My Dad kept it in his garage and took my Mom out for Sunday drives to keep it running well. That BMW was supposed to be my financial cushion if our marriage failed. At that point, it sunk in that Blaine had given me a financial cushion for a possible failed marriage. Should that not have been a red flag for me right there? I had sold the car to be able to purchase the fifth wheel for us to live in while we worked on the new business with my brother-in-law. Why did I give up my financial cushion? What propelled me to trust that the marriage would last and that I wouldn't need that cushion?

Since our divorce, Blaine and I had had many financial discussions that never went well. I had paid off one of his credit cards that he had defaulted on. I did it because my name was still on the account. This was before I had to default on all the other accounts and I was doing everything I could to keep my credit score up. I paid that account off with the money from one of the motorcycle sales. That sale was supposed to help me pay off the credit cards in my name and, instead, I was paying off one of Blaine's credit cards, just to save my credit score. I had even helped him with a down payment for his new Toyota truck from the proceeds of the sale on his motorcycle. He never paid me back for that down payment. I resented all of this and he had no idea why I was so angry.

I was furious with all the financial help that I had given him, while he failed to help me. I didn't receive any financial help in the divorce. I only walked away from the divorce with my own credit card debt. I had asked him to pay off one of my credit cards. He had agreed to make the monthly payment, but he was using the card as much as he was paying it off. Therefore, the balance stayed the same. The agreement was for him to pay off the card and he wasn't doing that. While this was a huge issue for me, he didn't feel any obligation to actually pay off this card. It was driving me crazy!

I realized that I needed to address this with him when I returned. While our friendship was solid, this financial issue was definitely going to drive us apart. Diane agreed that I needed to resolve this issue in order to keep the friendship with Blaine.

We continued on and ran across fields of long, vibrant red peppers and vineyards filled with luscious, purple grapes. The peppers reminded me of the peppers served the previous night at dinner.

There were detour signs that we had to follow part of the way through one of the towns because the flood waters made the way too muddy. We walked along a dirt trail that was full of mud and we had to be very careful where we stepped. I was afraid I was going to slip and end up with my rump in the mud! We sloshed along the muddy trail and the thick, red mud crept up over the toes and sides of my boots. Each time we got to drier ground, we would stomp our feet to get the clumped mud off of our boots to reduce the weight. We definitely did not want to carry any extra weight! This was a day that I was extremely happy to have hiking boots instead of hiking shoes or sandals.

We ran across a cool map of the continents on a hillside. The hillside was covered in brown dirt with green shrubs planted in the form of a map of the continents. It was amazing what we ran across along the way. We passed vineyards where we sampled a grape or two and found what looked like blueberries (but didn't taste like blueberries) along the winding pathway.

A short while later we laughed at one of the Camino signs. It was one of the bright blue signs with the Camino shell symbol, a hiker symbol, and a white arrow showing us the way. There were a few taxi advertisements attached to the sign. Tired of walking? Call a taxi! Good advertisement! Since we were only into our second day on the Camino, we did not even consider a taxi; it was something we might consider at a much later date.

In another village along the way, we stopped in a small town with two bars and got a Coca-cola zero along with a much-needed bathroom break. Our hike continued along fields of sunflowers and the tall yellow flowers made me smile. Beautiful! As we passed closer to the flowers, you could see that some of them had artistic features on them as pilgrims before us had removed sunflower seeds strategically to create a picture in the flower. I took a photo of one of the flowers with a heart shape on it.

Entering Villatuerta, we saw a lot of cleanup in the streets due to the flooding. The kids were cleaning up the deep mud and water on the tennis and basketball courts next to their school. A friend of mine said she had heard about some flooding in Spain and it appeared that we had run across it. We found our albergue, La Casa Magica, for the night and took off our boots as we waited to check in. The entrance floor was covered in cobblestones making it hard to walk on after taking off our muddy boots. Ouch!! During the check-in process, we opted to include the 4-course pilgrim's dinner for 13 Euros as well as breakfast in the morning for 5 Euros. Our passports were stamped with a bright red oval with what appeared to be St. James in the middle.

When we were shown our room, we were happy to see that there were only five beds per room with no bunks! It was worth the 12 Euros to not have bunk beds! We were the first ones in the room, so we had our pick of the beds. We selected beds on either side of the window. Each bed was covered with a white fitted sheet and contained a pillow encased in a white pillowcase. We pulled our sleep sacks onto our beds and put our own pillowcases over the pillows.

We lucked out in our first shared room! We ended up sharing the room with two Hungarian women in their 60s who spoke no English and another younger girl from China. It was nice to have our first shared room be one that was shared by all women.

We took our showers and Diane called over to me that she had forgotten her towel on her bed. I hurried to dry off and get dressed so I could bring the towel to her. At least I was there to get it for her as the bathrooms were co-ed. After the showers, we went to wash clothes. We were lucky enough to find an available washer so we threw our clothes in for a wash.

Finally ready to relax, we noticed that they had an excellent selection of beers. We each decided to try a different beer and then sat on the great terrace overlooking a courtyard. There were some colorful hammocks hung for relaxing in and a small area where a woman was doing yoga. We enjoyed the beer and internet while the clothes were washing. We noticed that there was a double sink that had a washing brush so we grabbed our boots and scrubbed the mud off of them. It was a relief to get the mud off of our boots! Once our clothes were done, we hung them up on the clotheslines in the courtyard below.

The kitchen had an open format and we could see them preparing our dinner for the evening. There were two guys cooking paella in a huge oval pan over an open flame. It really was a huge pan; must have been at least 3 feet long and full of paella. We enjoyed watching them cook and were getting very hungry for dinner at 7:00 p.m. Their cooking filled the lower level with incredible aromas.

When it was time for dinner, we walked into the dining area to colorful red and white checkered tablecloths on tables for four. We sat down with a couple and they introduced themselves as Dorothy and Lou from Arizona. It was fun chatting with them as we went through our four-course pilgrim's dinner. We started off with a Russian salad (potato salad) followed by vegetarian stuffed roasted red peppers. The main dish was a vegetarian paella which was amazing. The vegetables on my plate of paella started to look like a smiley face, so I rearranged them a little and added green beans as eyebrows and took a picture of my smiley face paella. We ended the meal with an excellent flan for dessert. As always, dinner was accompanied by scrumptious bread and they gave us two bottles of red wine for our table of four. It was an awesome dinner and a delightful evening!

We went to bed next to our open window. Thankfully, there were only five of us in the room, so it would be fairly quiet. As we lay in our beds in our first shared room, we listened to the neighborhood kids singing outside the window. How sweet! As I lay there, I chatted via WhatsApp with the guy who was my last date before my trip, enjoying the internet connection. It helped to have a little bit of ordinary home routine even though I was thousands of miles away. I was grateful that the room was indeed quiet. I lay there satisfied with our first two days on the Camino and was more confident that I would be able to accomplish the entire hike. I looked forward to what the next day would bring.

Steps: 30,907

The Journey Inward

Villatuerta – Los Arcos

Day 3 of 31 (September 2nd):
Kilometers: 25.3
Miles: 15.7

We started our day with our new routine which was quite simple. Most of the time we slept in the clothes that we were hiking in the next day, so we woke up dressed. With no makeup to put on, we quickly brushed our hair and teeth and then moved on to preparing our feet for the day. I had not worn makeup while living on the sailboat nor while on the motorcycle ride, so it was nice to have the comfort of the Camino bring me back to a natural "me" instead of the "made-up me". There was no judgement on the Camino.

I noticed that the side of one of my heels was getting a hot spot. My Darn Tough socks had been very comfortable; therefore, I was surprised to feel the hot spot. It was not yet a blister so I put a piece of my fancy paw print Bailey duct tape on it as suggested by the REI salesman.

Diane had started getting blisters on her toes on the first day, so she was spending a little more time each morning tending to her feet before putting her boots on. I was thankful that I had not been getting any and I hoped this hotspot would not develop into one.

Our room and bathroom were on the second floor and, as I looked out the bathroom window, I saw a gorgeous sunrise. The orange hues of the sunrise above the mountains lit up the feathery clouds against a bright blue sky. What really caught my attention were the several jet trails that crisscrossed along the sky and were brightly lit by the sunlight. So striking!

We started the day with breakfast at the albergue. It was a self-serve buffet with bread, yogurt, juice, coffee, and hard-boiled eggs. I was excited to see the eggs! It was wonderful to start with some protein for the morning; I was used to starting my day with a protein drink while staying away from carbohydrates. While the carbs were needed for the hike, the protein was a pleasant treat.

Our hike started with some ups and downs on the trail but it was not as rocky as the previous two days. As we headed out of town, we noticed a mountain range in the distance that had steep white cliffs on them. I remarked to Diane that it reminded me of the white cliffs of Dover. On the approach to the town of Estelle, we saw the cutest little grey and white donkey with preciously large ears sticking straight up. He was behind a fence next to the road. He made me smile. I stopped to say "Hi" to him.

We entered the town and passed a church with beautifully carved figures of different people along the top third of the church as well as a striking archway above the door with a variety of figures in it. The figures in that archway were very different, including an angel with wings, people with halos, and a strange head with its mouth open exposing a full set of straight teeth holding people sitting inside. They were very odd figures.

We wandered through town and ran across a delivery truck with the name Bimbo on it. It was parked in a small parking lot on the side of the road. We were not familiar with the Bimbo Bakery brand, so we had to laugh at the name. Diane couldn't resist posing next to the truck and pointing to herself....assuming the bimbo mentality. She always cracked me up and I loved her humor! We definitely were having a lot of fun together. I was grateful to be traveling with a great hiking buddy.

The Journey Inward

There was a dirt path that led out of town and we soon came upon the Irache Winery where the famous wine fountain resides. It is a fountain that has two spigots: one dispenses water and the other dispenses red wine! It was only around 9:30 in the morning, but we weren't going to pass up a sip of free wine. Besides, it was 5:00 somewhere!

We waited for our turn and were entertained by a group of 4-5 cyclists from Portugal who hammed it up for the camera and pretended to drink directly from the spigot. Many pilgrims use their scallop shell to take a sip of the wine, but our shells were already attached to our backpacks. We each emptied one of our water bottles and poured a little wine into the water bottle to sample. It was actually pretty tasty! Not sure of the type of wine, but I usually enjoy cabernets and I certainly enjoyed this wine. It was such a nice treat!

As we walked around the building I saw a sign which stated that we could get our pilgrim passport stamped with the wine stamp in their office, so we circled around to the other side of the building. We found their office and got our passport stamped with their Fuente del vino stamp.

We ran across our Hungarian friends again as we came out. We saw one go into the church across the street and then saw her friend come up the hill and was looking all over for her while calling out her name, "Edi...Edi...Edi." She didn't speak English so we had to use sign language to show her that her friend had gone inside the church. We looked pretty funny trying to tell her where her friend had gone! So now we knew the sturdy tomboyish Hungarian was Edi, but we never learned the name of the second woman who was all of 4'8" and could be found a mile or two behind her traveling companion on most days.

Our hike continued through many dirt paths wandering around the countryside of farms and pastures. We passed a grassy field where a shepherd and his black sheepdog watched over his herd of 20 to 30 sheep. He was wearing khaki shorts, a light blue polo shirt, and a white hat that reminded me of the hat that Gilligan wore on the TV show Gilligan's Island. He held a tall walking stick in each hand. There was no fence, so the sheep were grazing on the edge of our trail. I veered to the left a bit to avoid the sheep as not to disturb them.

We stopped in one of the towns for a quick break and to buy a drink. As we rested, we watched a cute kitten begging at the table next to us where two pilgrims were eating. They were kind enough to give the kitten something to nibble on. Diane attempted to contact the airline again to try to get her lost tripod case delivered to our next albergue. Frustratingly, the airline "lost and found" line was either busy or rang and rang and rang.

We knew we had a long final stretch so we were going to stop in the last town before that stretch to make sure we had plenty of water. Somehow, we walked right through a town without knowing it. Were we close enough to another town that we didn't see the difference? We kept looking for the town around the next corner, but it didn't come. Finally, another pilgrim we were walking with mentioned that we were on our final stretch! We were not prepared for it but were probably already a third of the way through it. We had hoped to stop for an extra bottle of water before we started the final stretch. The trail opened up into large, sunny fields with the trail meandering through them. It was extremely hot with no wind or shade and the trail just kept winding through the lonely fields. There were many flat, dusty, boring trails.

We passed a man walking with his donkey going the opposite direction. His donkey was loaded down heavily with a large pack on each side of him along with all types of other gear loaded on top. I wondered if that gentleman had walked his Camino to Santiago and now was walking back home. I would be lucky to walk just one direction of the Camino!

I became extremely tired halfway through our six-mile section and realized I was dehydrated. I rationed my water since we missed the last town where we would have purchased an extra bottle of water. There was very little shade. The blistering sun was beating down on me and I was slowing in the stifling heat. I was getting worried about not having enough water with me. We obviously were not prepared for this long stretch of desolate land. Diane was still a little ahead of me. I tried to get my iPod out to listen to music but realized that my headphones were buried and it would take more than a quick stop to find them. It was dangerously hot to stop for that, so I slogged on. I was overheated, frustrated and at my wit's end!

About two miles from our destination we finally found a shade tree to take a break. I still had no idea how much further we had to walk and could not see the town. I was slowly dragging to that shady spot.

I practically stumbled to our stop and plopped down for a rest. I chatted with another pilgrim who offered water. I declined the offer being hopeful I could make it to the next town. I berated myself for not being prepared and ensuring I had enough water for that part of the hike. I knew we had a long hike before our final stop. However, I was grateful to know this fellow pilgrim would have shared her water. I pulled out my earphones while resting so I could listen to music as a diversion for the rest of the way. After about 10 minutes, we reluctantly got up to finish our hike for the day.

My hiking buddy started ahead of me while I hooked up my iPod and tried to figure out how to select a song. Since it was a new iPod I was not familiar with it and couldn't find my playlists. I cursed myself for not being familiar with this new music app but didn't want to stop and get further behind. It was too sunny to see the screen so I finally saw albums and selected that. It was alphabetical, so AJ Croce appeared first on the list, but that wasn't peppy enough for my walk. Next up was Aerosmith! I selected them and randomly selected an album, Big Ones. Selected "Love in an Elevator" and I was off! The music was just the push I needed! I no longer trudged but walked at a very nice speed. I eventually caught up with my hiking buddy and passed her as she pushed to catch up with me. I watched her jaw drop and then she exclaimed: "Guess the music did it"? I shouted back "Aerosmith"! It was the perfect album with song after song being huge hits and I sang along as I trekked energetically to the town.

Thankfully nobody was walking near me to hear my off-key singing! It is amazing how powerful music can be! It was able to energize me and give me a second wind to help propel me to our destination.

Strangely we couldn't see the town until we turned the final corner and then it was only about a 1/4 mile away....an oasis in the middle of the desert! I was quite excited to see the town!

As soon as we entered the town there was a rest stop with vending machines that had my favorite Aquarius. I didn't stop with just one. I chugged down one and immediately got another. I felt so much better! I looked around for Diane and she was more interested in the black-haired twenty-something Spaniard standing nearby who looked like he could have just stepped out of a bullfight. I shook my head, laughing at her distraction, and got her attention to continue on our way. With sore feet and legs, we trudged into town and found an albergue. The heat had really taken a toll on me and I was exhausted. It felt wonderful to lay on that bed for a rest! At that point, I really didn't care about being clean but knew we would need to go through our afternoon routine of showering and washing our day's outfit before we could go to dinner.

After resting for about an hour, we reluctantly got up to take showers. We had to trek across a courtyard to get to the shower area. There were only two shower stalls. Thankfully, they were both available and we finally managed to get our showers.

Unfortunately, the internet was not working. One of the new pilgrims went to try to get that fixed.

After finishing an invigorating shower and washing our clothes by hand for the first time, we took to the street for dinner and found a great outdoor café serving a nice pilgrim's meal: an awesome salad, crusty bread, choice of entree, ice cream and vino! This would become routine for most of our meals.

The pilgrim's meal was common along the route. It normally consisted of a first course with a choice of soup, salad or pasta. That was followed by a second course which was usually a choice of meat accompanied by fries. The meal ended with a choice of dessert. The selections varied but often consisted of fruit, ice cream, and flan. The meal was always accompanied by wonderful, crusty bread and a bottle of red wine. This was much more food than I was used to eating for dinner, but after walking all day, it was always a welcomed dinner. I usually leaned toward low-carb meals, but I definitely needed the carbs to fuel my walks. The bread was always amazing and I enjoyed being able to savor it each day. It was nice to be able to eat anything I wanted and not worry about putting on weight. At least I hoped I would not gain weight after all that walking!

The outdoor café was very pleasant. We enjoyed the fresh air venue and all the great people watching it provided. An excellent way to end a very hard hiking day!

As we rose to leave, a gentleman asked us how our meal was and what we had eaten. He and his wife had just sat down at a table near us and were preparing to order. We chatted about our meal and then casually went back to our room. Little did I know that I had just been introduced to some of the magic of the Camino and that we would run into this couple again?

Our room had beds for six people and, thankfully, there were only three of us in the room. We chatted with our roommate when we returned and got along very well with her. She was a single woman from Maine who was celebrating her 60th birthday and was doing the Camino alone. Neither Diane nor I felt she was too motivated as she mentioned several times the idea of catching a bus to the next town although she had really just started. Diane and I both agreed that busing it would only be an option if one of us was physically incapable of walking for that day.

We chilled there for the evening and were grateful to have nobody else join us in that room. Thankfully they finally got their internet up and running so I was able to continue with my online journal. As I finished each online journal entry, I would tear out that day's section in my guidebook to slowly lighten the weight of that book.

Steps: 38,297

Los Arcos – Logrono

Day 4 of 31 (September 3rd):
Kilometers: 27.6
Miles: 17.1

As we prepared to leave the albergue, I went to grab my boots only to find only one pair left on the rack and they looked like my boots. As I was putting them on, they just did not feel right. They felt too big. I took them off and examined them. They were the same brand and style as my boots, but were the wrong size! I panicked as I realized someone else had taken my boots. Thoughts ran through my head trying to comprehend the situation. How would I get my boots back? If I couldn't, where could I find new boots? And I definitely did not want to be hiking this trail in brand new boots; I couldn't even imagine the blisters that would cause.

The lady who had shared our room with us was just putting on her boots and trying to figure out why they were too tight for her. I hadn't even seen her on the other side of the room. As I was alarmingly telling Diane that someone took my boots, the lady realized she had my boots. We quickly swapped and I had my beloved boots back. A huge wave of relief came over me as I sat down to put on my own boots.

We had to backtrack a bit back into town to find something for breakfast. We stopped by a small market and grabbed a cookie and an apple. I had no doubt that I would walk off the cookie! We headed out of town and began our long trek for the day.

After walking a couple of miles we saw our next town, Sansol, in the distance with a distinct church steeple rising up in the middle. We were surrounded by desolate, brown fields that looked like they once held crops but the road we walked was paved. The anticipation of achieving the next town began again. It was interesting that you would see this cluster of buildings in the distance and it would be totally surrounded by empty fields. It seemed like it would take forever to finally reach the town as it tempted you far away in the distance.

As we walked together, we started chatting about our online dating experiences. I had only been trying online dating for about six months, but Diane had been doing it for a few years. Both of us were very strong, independent women and we wondered if that made it harder to attract men. Were men put off by our independence?

We discussed how hard it was just to get to a first date. It would begin with emails via the online site and many email attempts coming in or going out with no matches. Eventually, there was mutual interest. Then, if both of you were enjoying getting to know each other via email, it progressed to texting. Many times it just didn't make it past the email or texting phase. Finally one of those conversations would lead to a first date. All that work just to get to a first date to meet in person and see if there was any chemistry. At that point the truth comes out; did they look like their pictures?

While we chatted about getting from texting to an actual date, I told her that I had learned to figure out which was the best way to text a guy. While some guys were fine reading a paragraph, I was running into many guys who would send multiple one line texts, one after the other, that would have fit nicely into a paragraph. If they texted like that, then I was better off texting back the same way. Texting a paragraph was just not effective to this type of guy. She laughed and said she never thought of that.

It seemed like I was having trouble getting past the first date. I had several first dates where there was just no chemistry. I told her about one of my first dates. He met me for a drink. Within 30 minutes, he had chugged down three beers and then said he needed to go. We had only been there for 30 minutes! I figured that he just wasn't attracted to me, so that was why he wanted to leave so early. Then he wanted to show me his new motorcycle. I knew I was never going to get on the back of his motorcycle if he drank like that! That was my fastest date ever! The funny part was he contacted me a few days later to go out again. Seems that he had plans for dinner with his daughter the evening we met for a drink which is why he left so quickly. After seeing how much he drank, I certainly was not going out with him again. Diane laughed at my story.

I told her about my date in Greenville, how well it went and that he was definitely worth a second date. She agreed with me that a long distance relationship would be difficult. I said that I finally made it to a second date with one guy, but when he mocked me on something I said to him, I knew there would be no third date. I could not imagine how he would act long-term if he already treated me like that on the second date!

While I was having a hard time getting past a first date, she told me about a guy that she met on Match. They met for coffee and hit it off but he never asked her out on another date. She started running into him at work and when she was out. They laughed that it was fate, but again he would never ask her out. He sat with her when she was having lunch. They'd sit in his car and talk and kiss. He would steal kisses in the elevator, but still never asked her out on an actual date. Eventually, she found out that he was seeing someone. She called him out on this since he had been telling her that he just wasn't ready to date. They had a big fight over that. During the first couple of days on the Camino, she had sent him a few pictures of our walk and he responded that he'd like to hear all about the trip when she got back. She was hoping this would finally lead to a date!

The Journey Inward

I told her about the one guy that I did date on and off for a few months. He kept stringing me along as well. I couldn't count the number of times that he canceled plans with me, always coming up with an excuse. I called him out on it many times. When he stood me up for my 50th birthday, I finally broke up with him for good. I realized that I deserved much better than that. I told her that she deserved much better than this guy who would not ask her out on a proper date.

She told me that she had been going out with another guy, but she had just ended the relationship before leaving for the Camino. She said he always seemed aloof and disinterested. Plus he hadn't been supportive of her trip to Spain. He told her that she should be spending her money on getting the roof replaced on her house, not hiking the Camino. We both agreed that it was a good thing that she broke up with him. I knew she loved to travel and this was definitely not the right guy to be with. First of all, he had no right telling her how to spend her own money. Secondly, she needed someone who understood the joys of travel!

We bantered around a couple more dating stories and I said that I wasn't sure that I wanted to continue to pursue online dating when I returned from the Camino. It was just so much work with not great results so far. She felt that she wanted to continue to give it a shot. We fell silent then; both of us reflected on our past dates and wondered what the future would hold.

In a remote part of our trail through a wooded section, we came across hundreds of tiny piles of rocks. Each pile consisted of 2-10 rocks piled on top of each other of various sizes, and some had notes left between the rocks. I have no idea what that meant. Wondering how in the world it got started and why pilgrims would continue to add other piles. It was really odd to see some of these things along the trail.

The countryside was still dotted with vineyards and orchards, so it was a pretty walk. We sampled fruit along the way when we passed close to it; we had already sampled grapes, blackberries, figs, and something that looked like a blueberry but definitely was not a blueberry. We had no clue what it was. Some of it was farmed and much of it was wild. We had fun tasting our way along The Way.

We finished our 4-mile hike to Sansol and took a quick break. We filled our water bottle from one of the many fountains along the way. The Camino provided water fountains in many of their small villages where you could fill your container with fresh, delicious water. They were usually available fairly often, so Diane and I carried a single water bottle which we continued to refill. During longer sections, we decided we would buy a second bottle to refill.

After wandering through forests and empty fields with no houses in sight, we completed our 6.5-mile stretch to Viana. We decided to stop for lunch. I ate my first bocadillo sandwich which is a six-inch section of awesome crusty French bread with meat, cheese or egg in it. Mine had a type of ham in it, like prosciutto ham, and thinly sliced tomatoes. It was mainly locals at the bar and restaurant and it was amazing the amount of wine being served at 2 pm!

We had found a table outside to relax and eat our lunch. I started eating my sandwich and wondered what was taking Diane so long inside. She finally came out with a large bowl and a basket of crusty bread. Her bowl contained a large salad with lettuce, eggs, tuna and large slices of tomato lining the perimeter of the bowl. As she enthusiastically started eating the salad, she raved over it saying it was the best salad she ever had. I honestly think that after hiking all of those miles the food just tasted better! It was a treasure after walking so far.

As we prepared to leave, Diane decided to put on her compression socks. They had the appearance of black knee-high nylons. She then put on her white hiking socks over the compression socks and they only went a third of the way up her calf. Finally, she donned her hiking boots. I said "Sexy!" and I just had to take a picture of her. She then posed in a stance that reminded me of Steve Martin's "wild and crazy guy" pose. She was always making me laugh along the way. Such a joy!!

The Journey Inward

I posted that picture later that day on Facebook and Diane's comment to the picture was "Do these socks make my butt look big?" She was so much fun to be around. I was lucky to have her as my walking buddy!

During our second stretch of six miles, we ran into our first rain. We found some trees to hide under as we managed to learn how to put the rain cover on our packs and don our raingear. Diane had a raincoat and I had opted for a poncho. It took me a while to figure out how to get it on. It only rained for a short while, and then it stopped. After a while, the poncho was getting very hot so I stopped and pulled it off. I folded it in two and draped it over the waist clip of my backpack so it would be ready if it started to rain again.

We laughed at two French Canadian men we had passed a couple days earlier because we passed them again and they pretended to play violin music as we passed. One of them remarked that he was a doctor of Gynecology, spoken in a heavy French accent, dripping with sarcasm. We ignored his remark and kept walking. A couple of minutes later they flagged down a passing van and got in to ride to the next town. I call that cheating!!

When we got into Logrono, we went to our first choice of albergues. We didn't like the neighborhood and, when we walked in, there was a group of locals at a table that stared at us as we assessed the albergue. It was extremely hot and somewhat smelly in there, and it just didn't feel right, so we looked at each other and made the choice to venture on to see what else we could find. We decided to simply trust our gut on this decision. If it didn't feel right, then we knew we needed to search for a different option. There had to be something else available out there. We kept walking through the big city hoping to find a comfortable place for the night.

We trekked to our second choice and they were full. The lady at the albergue called a pension (hotel) for us and they gave us a room for close to the same price as the albergue. She called us "chicas" while letting them know we needed a room. Haha! While she was trying to give us directions to the hotel, a Spanish gentleman came out and said "follow me" and then proceeded to escort us to the hotel. He wore jeans and a black shirt with a black pack slung over his shoulder. He was a little shorter than Diane as he walked next to her while I followed behind. He had black hair with just a little grey in his sideburns. He was a very sexy escort to our room for the night.

We ended up with a nice room for just a small amount more than the albergue and were very happy with it. We were exhausted and very thankful for the room. Our cute Spanish escort even helped us check in and brought us up to the room. It was very sweet of him to take care of us.

After a relaxing hot shower, we went out in search of dinner. We ran into the couple that we had met the day before who asked us about dinner. They were coming out of a restaurant as we were looking at the menu. Since this was the second time we had run into them, they introduced themselves and said they were from Sweden. His name was Lennart and he was very tall with a white beard and mustache and grey/white hair. He was very vibrant, energetic and cheerful. His wife introduced herself as Agneta but said we could call her Agnes (assuming since Agnes is a more common name.) She was closer to my height of 5'3", had a round, friendly face and short hair that was dark gray with a little bit of light gray around the front. She was quieter and more demure, but you could see her heart of gold sparkle in her eyes.

They highly recommended the restaurant and told us about the burgers they just had. We decided to give it a try. We were happy they recommended it because dinner was excellent. I had a huge hamburger with an excellent crusty bread bun. It was actually a really good burger. I had two glasses of wine with my burger and then both of us splurged on café con leches (coffee with milk) with some Baileys. The total of my bill for the burger, wine, and coffee with Baileys was only 10 Euros...just over $10!! While it is not common to tip in Spain, we always did. This evening we left a really good tip for our waitress and she was extremely grateful for it! She thanked us profusely.

The Journey Inward

While our days of walking were challenging, we always enjoyed our evenings! I guess my practice hikes were not so different than being out on the Camino. Always food-motivated hikes looking forward to that food and wine at the end of the day!

Steps: 38,777

Janet Charbonneau

Logrono – Najera

Day 5 of 31 (September 4th):
Kilometers: 29.6
Miles: 18.4

Refreshed from a nice hotel stay, we started walking out of the city. We got lost a couple times trying to follow the trail in the big city. Each time we got lost, a local would help us out. One time a lady whistled from across the street and pointed the correct way to us! The locals, our Camino angels, always seemed to be looking out for us!

    We hiked through an excellent hiking trail among the trees and grass in a park on the outskirts of the city. We passed many local people as they walked their dogs and biked through the peaceful trail. There was a lovely café surrounded by lush green grass that overlooked a beautiful lake just outside the park. It was a perfect place to stop for breakfast. We both had a tortilla Espanola and it sat upon an awesome piece of crusty bread. Wow, was it good! We enjoyed eating breakfast overlooking the peaceful setting.

    After breakfast, we continued our hike. Along the way we ran into the couple we had dinner with a couple of nights before and walked with them for a while. We even came across a pear tree and plucked a fresh pear for each of us. Boy, was it yummy! I only sampled the items deemed safe by me, such as grapes, blackberries, and pears, but Diane was always stopping to pick and eat things along the trail and

I warned her about the things she was not familiar with. I really didn't want to have to figure out how to get her to an emergency room in Spain! At one point someone cautioned her to make sure she picked the berries that were at least waist high, as it was a common occurrence for men to relieve themselves along the trails and waist high would be…"cleaner." Not something she had thought about, but definitely a good idea.

We ran across a small wooden structure where a man with long grey hair and a grey beard sat. Our hiking buddies knew of him and quickly went to chat with him. His name was Marcelino Lobato Castrillo. He had his own Camino stamp and we learned that he had been hiking the Camino since 1971. Often dressed in the medieval pilgrim outfit, he had hiked all of the Camino trails and often spoke in universities and conferences about the magic of the Camino. After he stamped our passports we chatted with him for a few minutes.

We stopped in Navarette for a quick drink and I bought a banana for a snack. We plodded on, making a quick stop at a picnic table outside of Ventosa. Outside of the rest area was a sign that said there were 593 kilometers to Santiago. Yes, we still had a lot of walking ahead of us!

When we got to Najera, the first albergue was full but we kept looking. We saw a sign for an albergue on a side street and walked over to it. As we were debating about going in, an attractive young gentleman, who looked like he was around 20, opened the door and asked if we wanted to stay. How do you say "no" to this sexy, young guy? He had a Russian accent and was very pleasant as he chatted about the albergue. He offered us a room with three beds and gave us the option of paying a little more to ensure that we would be the only occupants in the room or pay less with the possibility of someone coming to sleep on that third bed. We opted to take our chances and pay less; thankfully, no one took the third bed so we ended up in a private room with its own bathroom. How awesome!

They had a washer and dryer, so the cute guy running the place told us to bring our clothes out and he would put our clothes in the washer. Such wonderful service! We managed to get a load of clothes done in the washer/dryer which was a luxury! We ran across a couple whom we had met previously and they were planning to stay at the albergue and make their own meal in the sparse cooking arrangement. We decided to find a nice bar in town for dinner.

Once our laundry was done we were both very hungry. We wandered out into the town and found a quaint little bar that looked like it had a decent menu. I ordered a menu item called Huevos rotos which seemed to be a fairly common menu item along our hike. It was essentially a bowl of French fries topped with a couple pieces of ham and a fried egg on top. It was actually very good!

We walked back to the albergue and chatted about how awesome the day had been. From the wonderful park and breakfast to a pleasant chat with another hiking couple, including fresh pears, to finishing with a private room and a nice dinner. We hoped more days could end up like this one.

Steps: 38,509

Najera – Santo Domingo

Day 6 of 31 (September 5th):
Kilometers: 20.9
Miles: 13.0

We went looking for breakfast before beginning our daily hike. We walked back into town and browsed over a few bars. Nothing looked extremely inviting so we settled on going back to the same bar where we had eaten dinner the previous night. Each of us grabbed a delicious croissant and then headed out of town as we munched on our breakfast. Upon exiting the town we got confused on our route. Several other pilgrims stopped with us as we gathered together to figure out the route.

There was a white arrow (not yellow) on the route on the right going up a dirt path on the hillside, but no arrow at the intersection to indicate a right turn. Pilgrims went both ways and finally someone who went straight found another mark and yelled back to the rest of us, so we all gathered together on the correct route and wandered up the hill along another dirt path.

Our route took us through differing agriculture as we passed from vineyards into hay fields and across a small waterfall. The sound of the rushing water was very soothing. We even ran across some root vegetables planted alongside the path. As we were walking in between hay fields that had already been cut, we saw a bright red plane zoom in low overhead to say "hi" to us! He circled around and we all waved to him. That was a really cool sight! We started to see the stacks of baled hay that were a common sight in the movie *The Way*. Often people would stop to rest, have lunch, and maybe even take a nap on these hay fortresses.

On the outskirts of a village named Ciruena, we stopped briefly at a park that had cool cement lawn chairs. We passed a nice golf course in a remote village, which was a ghost town except for the golf course. It was really weird to see a golf course in the middle of nowhere. It seemed to be an attempt to drum up some form of tourist business. It appeared to be pretty vacant, so it didn't appear that they were very successful.

By the end of the day, my right knee was in excruciating pain! I hobbled slowly into Santo Domingo. We ended up staying at the albergue, Abadia Cistercience, which was run by Cistercian nuns. Of course, our assigned beds were up on the 3rd floor! It was an agonizing struggle for me to climb the stairs with my very painful knee!

We had one extremely small bathroom (toilet and shower) for the 12 of us staying up there to share. Diane ran out of water pressure during her shower and barely got rinsed off! I had to wait for my turn as there was a line forming for the shower. Thankfully, when I finally got a chance to shower I had water for the entire shower. It was a challenge to find a place to put my dry clothes while I showered.

We had a room with three beds and ended up sharing it with a girl from Poland. The room was very small and dark and we didn't want to spend much time there. Between the tiny bathroom, bare-bones bedroom, and my bad knee, it was a very trying place to stay.

We only had internet in the courtyard, so we sat there for a bit to catch up with email and Facebook updates. We found a sunny spot in the courtyard to try to stay warm. The warmth of the sun made my knee feel a little better. While sitting in the courtyard, we heard about a couple who had already gone home after less than a week on the trail. No matter how much my knee hurt I had come too far to give up so easily! I could not imagine leaving now. Even with my knee hurting to the point I wasn't sure I could walk any further, I felt stubborn and determined to finish my hike, even if I had to hobble all the way to Santiago.

After only six days on the Camino, Diane and I really needed to be able to stay in more private rooms. This albergue was very bleak and after a long walk, it was hard to stay in this horrible spot. While it was only 6 Euros to stay there, the accommodations were extremely dismal. This was the first place that didn't seem exceptionally clean. Diane said she didn't sleep well and was worried about bed bugs as there were sheets and bedspreads on the beds that didn't seem to be changed between guests.

I had created a GoFundMe page for my 50th birthday so I posted that page again asking my friends to donate to private rooms for us. I was hoping to get a little love from home! By the end of the day, I had a few donations to help us stay out of albergues like this one! My friends rocked!

I had budgeted around 30-35 Euros per day which would easily cover daily meals, drinks and an average albergue for the night. After this grim albergue, we decided that we wanted to splurge on private rooms a bit more often. The GoFundMe funds would allow us to stay in a few nicer places. I decided I was willing to go above my budget and cut into my savings in order to stay in a few more private rooms with Diane. We both agreed that more private rooms would be in our future.

We went out for a drink and dinner but realized none of the places served dinner until 7 pm. Instead, we found a bar and sat outside with our red wine. We ran into the couple from Arizona with whom we had dinner a couple of nights prior and the girl from Holland, Dorene, whom we had met before.

Our conversations turned to relationships as Don and Lou had been married for more than 25 years. We talked about the pros and cons of being strong minded single women and finding a compatible life partner. We felt that our independence had a tendency to scare men away; yet we were happy to be able to be that independent and self-sufficient. As our debate continued, the cold was starting to bother my knee again, so I bought a second glass of wine, trying to numb the pain.

We headed back to the albergue to warm up in the sun in the courtyard until it was time for dinner. I hobbled as I walked because the knee was really hurting and all that wine had not numbed the pain! Sitting in the sun did indeed help it a little.

Dorene decided to join us for dinner. She was a striking woman, tall and slender with long blonde hair. She was a physical therapist and was married with young children. She had tried to walk the Camino previously but had to quit due to foot problems. Her husband encouraged and supported her desire to try again, so there she was. We found an interesting restaurant and had an excellent pilgrim's dinner. We were the only patrons there. We had a cute young waiter who spoke English and had a really fun time at dinner. For dessert, he started to list the options and he listed himself as the first dessert option...then he listed the real options. Ha! He was such a flirt!

It was cold when we walked back to the albergue. My right knee was screaming in pain and I barely made it up the two steep flights of cold, dark, uneven stone steps in the dimly lit stairwell to the room. Our young Polish roommate, Paulina, was already asleep when we got there. As I lay in bed, I wished I had something stronger that would help my knee. The ibuprofen was not enough to get rid of the pain. I cried myself to sleep not sure how I was going to walk in the morning.

Steps: 26,185

The Journey Inward

Santo Domingo – Belorado

Day 7 of 31 (September 6th):
Kilometers: 22.9
Miles: 14.2

We had to be out by 7:45 a.m. so we gathered everything quickly and went to the first floor to put on our boots. As I went to buy an Aquarius from the vending machine, I had to laugh that the Aquarius was 1.20 Euros and the San Miguel beer was only 1 Euro! Maybe I should change to beer! It might make my knee feel better!

We walked through wheat fields that had already been harvested. We stopped for breakfast in Azofra which consisted of crusty bread with egg, tomato, bacon, mayo, ketchup, and lettuce. It was really good and we had a cute orange tabby kitten come over for some scraps.

Later, we were walking along rolling hills and I heard a man behind me bellow, "I am Spartacus!" as he crested the top of the hill we were now descending. I turned around to look at who had made this declaration. He was hilarious. As he walked down the hill past us he said, "No one else is that old." We chuckled as he sped past us. It was nice to enjoy the humor as we trudged on our daily walk.

As we walked through the day, we kept getting passed by a German mom and her teenage daughter who constantly made "tic tic tic" sounds with their walking sticks...almost a dragging sound.

Diane named them "click n clack". You could hear them coming from behind and instantly knew it was them from the sound and cadence. I am glad my walking partner did not clack like that every day!

When we got to Belorado, the first two albergues that we went to were full. After making several phone calls and trying to speak to someone in Spanish, we managed to get a hotel room in a pension that was attached to an albergue. Thankfully Diane knew a little Spanish and was able to book this room. We waited for a lady to meet us and let us into the pension. We ended up with a decent private room with a shared bath next to our room. Unfortunately, this was another evening with no internet in our room.

We had our laundry washed and then we carefully hung it on the line to dry outside the window of our third story sitting area. We headed around the corner for drinks to wait until they started serving dinner. We eventually were directed to a table upstairs where we were served a satisfying pilgrim's meal. When we arrived back at the hotel we went to go get our clothes from the line. Diane was unpinning one of my shirts when the clothespin pinched her and she dropped my shirt on the ground...inside the albergue courtyard to which we did not have a key to access it! Ack! Diane went down and knocked on the albergue door and the people on the other side did not speak English and would not open the door! After trying for a while she gave up and came back up.

I was afraid of waiting until morning in case someone else took it, leaving me with only one walking shirt. I told her I didn't want to wait until the morning to attempt to get my shirt so I went down to the albergue door. Thankfully the manager was talking to the people in the albergue who had complained about the interruption (it was only around 9:00 p.m.) and I was able to signal to her that I had dropped my shirt and showed her my key to the room. She didn't speak English and I didn't speak Spanish, so I asked via hand gestures to be let into the courtyard. She reprimanded me. All I could say was "Muchos gracias" for letting me in and "pardon" which means "excuse me" since I did not know how to say I was sorry in Spanish.

The Journey Inward

Oh well, at least I got my shirt back!! I was proud because I had stayed strong and insistent. The Camino was bringing out the inner strength in me.

Steps: 31,422

Janet Charbonneau

Belorado – San Juan de Ortega

Day 8 of 31 (September 7th):
Kilometers: 24.1
Miles: 15.0

There was a festival the day before, and people had been singing in the streets until 4 in the morning. As we were walking out of town around 8 am, there were still guys in the streets drinking from the night before! One of them spewed Spanish and then in English said, "Have fun!" Diane and I just laughed as we passed them.

I already had my knee brace on my right knee to prepare it for the day. I took 4 ibuprofen before we left the albergue so, hopefully, I would kill the pain before it got unbearable. It was still a daily concern for me because I was not sure I would make it to Santiago. I desperately did not want to quit, so my stubborn self kept going.

Our first part of the daily hike was on dirt paths through vast wheat fields that had already been harvested. We entered Villafranca Montes de Oca and looked for a place to get a drink and snack. As we came up to a café, we ran across two dogs; one of them was a Golden Retriever. I went over to pet him and take a quick video of that cute wagging Goldie tail. It made me miss my two Golden Retrievers, Max and Bailey, and want to get another one soon. I wondered if I was ready for the responsibility of another dog yet.

The Journey Inward

As we left Villafranca, we began to enter the Oca Mountains where the gravel path was surrounded by green trees instead of the barren fields we had been hiking through earlier. We had very long ups and downs...some hills just seemed to go forever and you didn't know when you would reach the top! Diane dubbed the day "That Damn Blaine" day as it was his idea to do this trip and he wasn't there to enjoy the killer hills.

With my knee still bothering me, I could not go up and down too fast; it was frustrating to watch so many people pass me! One of the pilgrims passed me, saw my knee in a brace, gave me encouragement and told me to be patient and walk slowly. As I watched her disappear in the distance in front of me, I stopped and broke down in tears. This walk was so difficult for me with this painful knee. I really didn't know if I was going to make it another 23-24 days. I didn't want to come this far to quit, so my tenacity kept me going. I was determined to finish!

That pilgrim's encouragement was exactly what I needed. It was a reminder that this was not a race and I needed to walk the Camino at my speed...whatever speed would allow me to make it to the end with my hurting knee. I was doing the best I could and I needed to be satisfied with that. I started taking my time on those hard hills to make sure I didn't hurt my knee more. I think that was good advice for my painful knee, but was also good advice in general. I should learn to do things at my own speed and not care what others around me were doing.

When we got into town, there were only two places to stay and only one was an albergue. The guidebook said the population was 20 and there were 70 beds in this albergue, so the pilgrims were almost triple the population of the town. The albergue was a former monastery and there were three large rooms with rows of bunk beds covered in either bright blue or neon green sheets. We snagged a bunk bed in the first room and then realized that there were still plenty of beds in the next room. We managed to find two bottom bunks which, of course, meant a stranger was sleeping above you in the upper bunk.

We each found a hot shower (one of them said cold water only) and then went down and sat by a little fireplace to warm up. Again, there was beer available in the vending machine. You have to love beer in a vending machine! The funny thing was there was no place to put money in that vending machine. I looked all over to find out where to put my money. I wanted a beer! I finally figured it out. You had to put money in the coffee machine next to it and then press the appropriate two letters for the item in the drink machine. There wasn't a sign explaining that and it was really confusing!

As we sat by the fire trying to stay warm, a young guy came and sat at a table next to us. He was cute with tanned skin, black hair and a mustache with a goatee. He wore shorts, a casual button-down shirt, and a baseball cap. He took out his guitar and started playing. A few of us gathered around to listen to him. After he played a few songs I noticed that he had enticed a crowd of around 15 to listen to him. It was really cool and we had a very diverse crowd gathered of different ages and nationalities.

We didn't have internet again, but they had two desktop computers where we could connect to the internet. I got on Facebook and was really upset by what one of my friends had posted. A day earlier I had posted a link to my GoFundMe site that I had set up for my birthday. I had stated that we were already tired of staying in the albergues and would appreciate it if anybody wanted to donate a little to help us get more private rooms along the way. This friend came back and said that she didn't want to donate because we should be staying in the albergues to get the true pilgrim experience. Her comment implied that we should suffer along the way. I was furious. If she didn't want to donate to help us that was fine, but to make a remark like that was just plain mean! As far as we were concerned, we felt that we were there doing it and that "suffering" means different things to different people.

The Journey Inward

I responded to her comment and told her that all of us out there were true pilgrims. It didn't matter if you stayed in albergues the whole time or stayed in private rooms. It didn't matter if you sent your backpack ahead or carried it the entire way. I was hiking 12 to 19 miles a day and that made me a true pilgrim! So if I wanted a nice room at the end of the day then I deserved it! Just like in the movie The Way, we had similar discussions with other pilgrims on what a true pilgrim is. Every pilgrim we shared this story with was also upset by the comments made and agreed with me that unless you are there hiking the Camino, then you really didn't have the right to comment on where a pilgrim should stay or what they should do.

I was starting to discover that the Facebook comments were like little cheerleaders along The Way. Each encouraging comment helped propel me a little further. So upon receiving a comment that promoted my suffering to be a true pilgrim, I was frustrated. What I didn't realize is that I had not shared enough of my suffering for them to understand how difficult this really was.

The time finally came for dinner and I was really hungry. We had an awesome pilgrim's meal which consisted of soup, pasta, pork, fries, bread, and salad. Wine didn't come with dinner, but they did sell bottles so I bought a bottle of red wine for Diane and me for only 4 Euros. Dinner was served cafeteria style by local church women and we sat at very long tables with many others. It was really tasty and filling since there was so much included!

After dinner, we visited the beautiful old church next door. We came back to our room to find that they had brought mattresses into our room for many of the bicyclists since there were no beds left at the albergue. These guys were bicycling the Camino instead of walking it. Since they were bicycling, they usually were a lower priority at albergues than the pilgrims that were hiking on foot. They had bicycled up to the next town, Ages, and there was nowhere for them to stay so they shuttled them all back to San Juan de Ortega.

There were mattresses all over the floor of our room making it hard to walk around to your bunk. We now had 20 male bikers in our room. Wow, was it crowded! Thank God for earplugs! That was the only thing that was going to drown out all the snoring in this packed room.

Steps: 38,477

San Juan de Ortega – Burgos

Day 9 of 31 (September 8th):
Kilometers: 25.9
Miles: 16.1

As we prepared to start our day, I noticed a couple of blisters on the back of my ankle. I knew it was because I was favoring my bad knee and was walking oddly. The pain was excruciating when I bent my knee, so I was trying to walk by swinging my straight right leg around for the next step instead of bending the knee. My weird gait had caused me to have a couple of blisters. I finally understood what Diane was experiencing. She continued to get more blisters each day and spent about 10-15 minutes each morning prepping her blisters for the walk. I had to do that to mine this morning.

It was a very clear and cold morning. It was dark when we started and you could still see the stars. We kept hearing the faint sound of a bell coming from ahead. Soon we came across random cows grazing freely. We even had to wait for a few of them to cross the road before we could pass. They were bigger than us! One of them just stood in the middle of the road for a bit. Diane laughed that a girl from Wisconsin couldn't get away from cows, even in Spain. We also spotted a prayer labyrinth within the grassy field. It was a large spiral path with tall grass or straw sticking out to define the path to the center of the circle and it had a pile of rocks in the very center. It was meant to allow you to walk along the path to the center of the circle and then turn around and spiral back out, thus allowing you to walk and pray without getting lost.

We came upon a very, very, long steep uphill climb and then a steep descent. It was so rocky that it was very difficult to walk. Midway up I was cursing the movie *The Way* for not showing these types of routes in the movie. Every time they were walking, it was a nice smooth road and most of what I had seen so far had been full of rocks! Even most of the cyclists walked their bikes during this section. At the crest of the hill, there was a very large wooden cross and some of the bikers had stopped to take their picture standing as a group in front of the cross.

Near the cross, someone had taken the time to build a Camino arrow marker with stones on the ground along our path. It was at least 12 feet by 6 feet.

At our second town, we finally found a café open to buy something to eat for breakfast. We had to laugh at our Hungarian friend, Edi, who was drinking red wine with her breakfast! Diane and I both thought that 9 am was a bit early for red wine. We ended up splitting a bocadilla, while Diane enjoyed her café con leche and I enjoyed fresh orange juice. I was getting spoiled with the fresh squeezed orange juice that was available. Most bars had a machine called a Zummo and it took fresh oranges and squeezed the juice out of them. Therefore, when I asked for an orange juice, it was essentially made from the juice of three fresh oranges. It was delightful!

We continued on through the barren, rocky terrain. As we walked into one of the towns, we turned the corner to see a crumbling bell tower and Diane said, "that is how I feel"! I knew exactly how she felt...we all felt like we were falling apart out here! The physical challenge of the journey was definitely at its peak. Diane continued to suffer from multiple blisters on her toes and my knee ended up being painful every day. Our bodies were physically tired as well.

Our plan was to take an alternative route that would take us through a forest along a river into Burgos. We saw one arrow pointing to the river route but then missed the route somehow after crossing the highway. We didn't realize until we were on the wrong side of a small airport, so we slogged on along the hot asphalt. We walked along the hot streets through Villafria and past all the industrial buildings leading into Burgos. It was very long and hot and seemed to be drawn out forever! The cement was taking its toll on our feet and lower backs. We were sorry we had not backtracked to find the cooler, shaded river route.

We finally crossed into Burgos and got lost. We stopped at a bar and asked about the hotel we booked and the young woman behind the counter couldn't find it in the city on her phone. It must have been a suburb with the same name as the street we thought it was on. Thankfully, we didn't have a credit card attached to this reservation, so we didn't lose anything by not finding it. The bartender pointed us back to The Way and we went looking for a place to sleep. We passed a police station and, just outside, a very nice young man stopped to offer us assistance. The best he could do was point us in the direction of where there might be some lodging. I was so hot, tired, and thirsty that I really wanted to find a place quickly! I was disappointed that we had not stopped longer at that bar for something to drink.

We checked a few albergues and hostels and they were all full so we wandered looking for hotels. We found one with a small double bed. We asked to take a look at the room to see how small the bed was. It was pretty small so we decided to keep looking. After several more booked hotels and finding out there was an event in the city, we went back and booked that double bed. It was expensive, 75 Euros, but I used money from my GoFundMe account to pay for the room for us. Diane opted to use a couple of fluffy blankets as a bed instead. The bathroom was as big as the bedroom and we were happy it had a tub! We had a place to sleep and a hot bath! Heaven!

We learned that there was an international cycling race; therefore, almost every available bed in the city was taken. That also explained why the cyclists from the night before had turned back to settle for a mattress on the floor of our albergue.

There was a Pharmacia across from the hotel and we stocked up on needed items. I bought a knee brace for my left knee since it was busy compensating for my right knee already in a brace. I stocked up on ibuprofen which came in 600 mg! I had been taking four 200 mg pills, so this would lessen the number of pills that I had to carry. I also bought Compeed for the blisters on the back of my ankle.

We went back to the room to relax until it was time for dinner. Diane took a nice, long hot bath while I chatted with Blaine via WhatsApp. I told him how painful my knee was and that I didn't know if I was going to be able to finish the walk. I had started walking without bending my right knee, so my left knee was starting to take a toll from it. He suggested that if I could find Tiger Balm to buy it. I had just seen it at the Pharmacia, so I told him I would purchase it. He gave me encouragement which really helped. I needed that small amount of cheerleading to keep me going.

After my shower, we left to go find some dinner. On the way, I popped into the Pharmacia again to purchase the Tiger Balm that Blaine recommended.

We found a nice bar with a small high-top table and two chairs outside. I went in to get drinks and Diane wanted a Bombay and tonic. They took out a huge glass and put a few boulder-sized ice cubes in it. The bartender poured a lot of gin in the glass (it was a really good pour) and then opened a single-serve bottle of tonic and poured it down a bar spoon into the glass. How impressive! It was quite a big drink for Diane! I stuck with my red wine and we ended up enjoying a couple of drinks and a nice dinner at our outside table. The ambiance of Burgos nightlife was that of narrow alley-like streets lined with shops and restaurants. Families and lovers were strolling along on the perfect evening.

Steps: 43,981

The Journey Inward

Burgos – Hornillos del Camino

Day 10 of 31 (September 9th):
Kilometers: 20.8
Miles: 13.0

I woke up refreshed and realized that my knee did not hurt. The Tiger Balm worked! This was the first time in days that I thought I could actually finish the hike. I hoped that I would continue to have a pain-free walk the rest of the day.

There was a breakfast buffet included in our room price, so we went down to have some breakfast. As we walked in, we could smell the fresh coffee and bacon. I was extremely excited to have eggs for breakfast again. Eggs, bacon, awesome bread, fresh orange juice, coffee, fresh fruit.... it was delicious! While it sounds like a usual breakfast buffet back home, it was such a treat for us. After so many mornings of juice and toast, it was heaven!

We were starting the Meseta today which was a section of the Camino that was flat with few trees. It was said to be a boring section of the Camino. While I was happy to finally have flat sections to travel which would be easier on my knee, I was not looking forward to this bleak section.

After a late start around 9:30 a.m., we headed out of Burgos. Working our way through town, we came around a corner and encountered Our Lady of Burgos cathedral. It was massive and awe-inspiring with amazing artistry and architecture. We also saw tons of media that had set up to cover the race and the blessing of the cyclists that was due to happen that morning. We got lost heading out of town. We finally found the correct route only to get lost once again in the outskirts of Burgos in a construction area. We finally found our arrows to continue on our way.

We went through a couple of cute towns and ran into our friend, Dorene, in the second one. She went to the doctor to get her legs checked out and stopped early for the day. In the last town before our destination, we saw a couple of albergues. I saw a guy chase a mean cat away from others near one of the albergues. It looked like a quaint town and I almost suggested stopping there, but I wanted to accomplish more miles for the day.

We then went through a long uphill stretch that never seemed to end with 15-20 mph winds in our face. I was wondering why I didn't stop in that last town! Finally, we got to the top of the mountain and reached a very steep downhill stretch. Then it became very flat. The Meseta had definitely begun. We could see the town ahead, but it was deceiving. It looked like it was only a mile away, but it was closer to 2-3 miles. I kept my head down as the strong winds continued to blow against us and plodded along the flat terrain.

I raised my head to look across the barren landscape. The wind pummeled my face as I looked off to the left at one lone tree, standing so isolated. It looked out of place. There were no other trees nearby. It stood solid and strong, all by itself. I envied the tree because it was able to thrive by itself without being in a forest with other trees. At that point, I wanted to be like that tree…single and strong. I felt the tears streak down my face. Instead of single and strong, I felt alone and broken. The years since my separation and divorce had taken a toll on me. I took a picture of that tree as a reminder of what I wanted to become.

Upon entering Hornillos del Camino, we found two albergues and a hostel full. We ended up at the municipal albergue for 6 Euros. They provided us with disposable plastic sheets to cover the bed and the showers were wonderfully hot. Diane did her laundry by hand outside the back of the building. She said that there were swarms of biting flies that were unbearable. One young man that we learned was contemplating becoming a priest was also doing his laundry and he didn't flinch even once when there were up to 10 flies on his legs and arms. Diane was amazed.

Again, there was no internet, so I used my data package on my phone for a quick update. I wanted my family and friends to know we were safe for the night and in which town we were staying.

As we walked out of our albergue to go find something for dinner, we saw a gentleman sitting outside and playing his guitar. We stopped to listen to him for a few minutes. We wandered around the corner and found a quaint little bar for dinner. The chef was late. We said, "if you have wine and bread, we are happy," so they brought us a bottle of red wine and a basket of bread and we were happy to wait for the chef! I had an excellent stewed chicken in ale sauce. It was worth the wait!

While eating our salads, we saw the Swedish couple come and sit down at the table next to us. We chatted about our day and told them about our wonderful breakfast. Lennart was so jealous that he used his hand in a hand signal like a hand puppet (opening his thumb and fingers to represent an open mouth and then closing them to represent a closed mouth) and said, "Shut up"! He was hilarious! We have joked about his hand signal ever since, "Shut up, shut up!" *hand puppet motion* Too funny!

As we got ready for bed, I again massaged the Tiger Balm into my knee. It had kept me pain-free for the day, so I decided to continue using it. I was starting to feel confident that I would be able to make it to Santiago.

Steps: 35,029

Janet Charbonneau

Hornillos del Camino – Castrojeriz

Day 11 of 31 (September 10th):
Kilometers: 20
Miles: 12.4

We had two long stretches for the day with no real towns. I had read the distances and towns in my guidebook earlier that day so I was expecting a town in the middle of this first stretch and I kept waiting for it. I completely missed it! It consisted of one building. We passed it and I didn't realize it was the town! I kept looking for the town to come up until Diane told me we passed it! We continued to walk next to the many fields of cut wheat.

We finally got to the next town, Hontonas, for breakfast. There was a nice café with many tables outside on the green grass. It was a delight to see the luscious green grass in the middle of the rocky barren fields that we had been traveling through. We had free wifi and I got some very good news from home. As I sat eating my breakfast, I checked on Facebook and saw a pic from my sister of wine with lunch celebrating good news.

Anticipating the good news, I quickly checked my iPod for messages. I had been relying on Facebook messenger, so hadn't thought of checking my iPod messages at each stop with wifi even though I knew my sister was using that for communication. My fingers were shaking as I put the wifi password into my iPod to get the message. She said my Mom had a good follow-up checkup from her surgery the prior year and she wouldn't have to go back for any more follow-up checkups! I immediately relaxed with great relief and, as the news sank in, my eyes started welling with tears.

Diane looked at me with a worried look and all I could manage to say was, "happy tears." Once I had finally composed myself and wiped my tears away, I recounted to Diane the events of the past 9 months.

I told her about how my Mom had surgery the previous November. It was the day before Thanksgiving, so I planned to spend my Thanksgiving holiday up in Goldsboro, NC in order to help. My Mom was 89 and she had to have part of her colon removed. My two sisters and I planned to rotate the time needed to take care of Mom after surgery. Thankfully, the surgery went very well. One of my sisters spent the first night with her and when I went to relieve her the next morning, she told me that Mom had ripped out one of her IVs during the night.

I spent the next day and night with her. I was so concerned that she would rip out her IV, or something else attached to her, that I was a nervous wreck. It was Thanksgiving Day and I missed the turkey dinner with my family, so I could take care of my Mom. My nieces came up for a visit to allow me to take a break and eat a mid-afternoon turkey meal in the hospital cafeteria. My sister, who had cooked the turkey dinner for the family, brought a turkey sandwich for me.

That evening my Mom slept very little. She kept waking up and trying to pull things off of her. Several times she tried to get out of bed to go do really off the wall things. I would ask her why she was getting out of bed and she would say some strange thing like "I am trying to put the bacon in the freezer." She was delusional and talking about really random things which made no sense. Many times she asked why she was in a closet. We had strange discussions about flour, boyfriends (wasn't sure if it was mine or hers), hamburgers and ice cream. I finally started making notes about what she was saying so that I could relay them to her later.

I was really starting to worry about her delirious actions and words when I asked a nurse about it. She told me that it sounded like sundowners syndrome, so I looked that up on my tablet. That was exactly what it was and I felt a little better at that point. I wish they had given us a heads up before the surgery that this was a possibility after surgery. Evidently, it is fairly common for older patients who are used to a routine to experience this once the sun goes down. It makes them delirious and they do things that make no sense or are way out of character for them. I prayed that this was temporary. I was starting to understand how difficult it would be to deal with someone with Alzheimer's. I found things that would help her to get back into a routine like opening up the blinds during the day so she could see the daylight and know it was daytime.

At about 3 AM, she finally went to sleep for an hour. I got a chance to relax and found that I was starving. I ate that Thanksgiving meal in the cafeteria in the mid-afternoon and no dinner later on. Remembering that I had that wonderful turkey sandwich from my sister, I reached over for it and managed to enjoy a bit of homemade goodness for my Thanksgiving. I was extremely grateful that she had brought it because I didn't want to leave my Mom alone for even a minute to go get something to eat. While Mom became restless again, she seemed a little better. As the day dawned, she started to improve with each passing hour.

Thankfully, after a few days, she had improved and was released from the hospital. It took her a couple of months to recover, but I was thankful that one of my sisters lived with her and could take care of her during her recovery process. She reached her 90th birthday the next March and was doing well, but she had to go back to the doctor often for them to monitor her progress. She seemed to be progressing well, but every time the doctor wanted to see her for one more visit, we knew she was not out of the woods yet.

While on the Camino so far, every time we went into a church where they had candles to light I had lit a candle and said a prayer for my Mom. After 9 months of worrying about her recovery, it was such an awesome relief to get the news from my sister that she needed no more follow-up visits! When the doctor no longer needs follow-up appointments, then you know things are better! My Camino prayers had been answered! It made the rest of the day easier to walk...one less burdensome worry weighing me down.

The clouds disappeared and the day grew hot. We stopped at the ruins of a convent where there was an albergue. We peeked in to see it. It had no electricity and no hot showers. They ate dinner by candlelight. It would have been a neat experience except, after a hot day, we wanted a nice shower, electricity, and to be able to do some laundry. We kept walking to the next town.

We entered Castrogeriz and walked to the middle to find our albergue. We left our laundry to be done at the albergue and went into town to find an ATM and Pharmacia. I tried to pull out cash at the ATM and it came back with an error. I didn't know if there was something wrong with my account or the ATM. I was hoping my account was OK but I began to panic. I didn't want the machine to keep my card. I had the phone number of one of the guys at my bank back home so I called him to check. He said everything looked fine and that it looked like it had attempted to pull money from a savings account which did not exist. While I was talking to him I came across another ATM. Wow, was I grateful! I managed to successfully withdraw more money. I thanked him for checking my account for me. We then looked for the Pharmacia and it was closed for siesta time.

We stopped at a bar for Sangrias. It had a nice outdoor seating area overlooking the countryside. I went inside to the bar to order our drinks. I watched the bartender as she pulled out two huge glasses and added a few large ice cubes to each glass. She made the sangria from scratch with red wine, brown cane sugar, and a white wine/liquor and then topped it with orange soda. She garnished both of them with orange slices. They were definitely a bargain at three Euros each! I brought them outside to the table where Diane was sitting and we took a sip of this heavenly concoction. It was delicious!!

We always enjoyed the afternoons when we were done walking and could celebrate our accomplishment of the day with savory wine or scrumptious sangrias.

On the way back to our albergue, we ran into our Swedish friends who were traveling with a woman who was a hospital executive from Taiwan. We decided to join them back at the bar for drinks and dinner. We all had sangrias, since ours were so good earlier, and sat out on the terrace overlooking the peaceful mountains in the distance with wind turbines on top of them. Diane ran back to check on our laundry and put it in our room. Then she came back to join us with our sangrias.

When it was time for dinner, we moved inside to eat. We had a fun and delicious dinner. I had a phenomenal steak and whiskey cake for dessert. We had to laugh at Lennart because one of the dessert choices was lemon mousse. He misheard it and said, "moose lips?" We got so tickled at him. The waiter got so caught up in our laughter, that he told the table next to us that there were moose lips for dessert. He immediately realized his mistake, corrected himself, and announced, "lemon mousse." Our entire table burst into laughter when we heard him announce mouse lips for dessert!

Our waiter's name was Alejandro! Diane finally met Alejandro...an inside joke for us. Since we had both been trying out the online dating scene with no luck, Diane had joked before we left for the trip that maybe we would meet Alejandro and Mateo. When our waiter introduced himself as Alejandro, Diane and I looked at each other and laughed at our inside joke. Alejandro was a cutie and I took a picture of him with Diane as we were leaving.

I had been feeling very tired all day so the bed was a welcome sight at the end of the day! Unfortunately, I was on a top bunk over a lady who I did not know, so I tried to stay put and not climb up and down too many times. Diane was also unfortunate to be in the top bunk above a woman with a terrible cold who coughed and blew her nose all night. Everyone seemed to already be in bed, so we had to quietly get ourselves ready. Needless to say, neither of us slept well.

The Journey Inward

Steps: 35,132

Castrojeriz – Boadilla del Camino

Day 12 of 31 (September 11th):
Kilometers: 19.1
Miles: 11.9

Some pilgrims were up at 5:30 a.m. getting ready for the day. We slept in a little longer since we planned to leave at 8:00. At 7:45 a.m. the albergue's manager was telling everyone that they had to be out by 8:00 a.m.! Good grief! Can I at least get my boots on before you throw me out the door? Another pilgrim that had stayed the night in a different room pulled up her sleeves to show Diane a line of small red welts. Bedbugs!!! The woman told the albergue owner and he vehemently denied that there could be bed bugs at his place! He asked the woman to show him what bed she had slept in. Luckily, we didn't have any problems.

Diane had expressed her fears about bedbugs often, so she was definitely more proactive at looking at all her beds to make sure there was no evidence of bedbugs. It was a problem that existed on the Camino and I had read of others who had to wash everything they were carrying to get rid of them. Both Diane and I had been proactive before we left for our trip. We both treated our silk sleep sacks and the outsides of our backpacks with permethrin. It was either working well or we had been really lucky since we hadn't had a bed bug problem.

The Journey Inward

We walked along rolling hills of cut hay; it was a boring walk. We had a very long uphill climb, followed by another never-ending uphill with an 18% incline downhill on the backside. It was extremely difficult walking downhill with my hurting knees! I had to take it really, really slow. It was very frustrating! While the Tiger Balm helped me wake up pain-free, the steep descents were still painful on my knees. Thankfully the Tiger Balm was at least making it bearable.

I was grateful that the path evened out and I had a chance to catch up to Diane. I did well with flat terrain. We walked along a section next to a river which was muddy brown with some sort of reedy plant sprouting out on the edges. There were trees next to the river and some of their leaves were turning yellow. It was such a tranquil walk. I missed being near the water since I love water so much. It made the walk quite peaceful and soothing.

The smell of pear trees greeted us as we entered the next town. The aroma made my mouth water. We passed a brick and stone building that had beautiful wrought iron in front of the windows and window boxes full of bright red, pink and white flowers. It was very striking! We stopped in the small town of Itero de Vega for lunch. I had a burger and fries. It was OK but not as good as what I am used to eating. I really missed a good juicy burger like we had back home.

It had been a nice cool walk before lunch, but, when we got back on the road, it became a hot barren walk. There wasn't any shade for any relief from the sun. It was amazing the difference between the cool morning and the horrible, hot afternoon. We just kept trudging along in the hot sun, dreaming of our stop for the night. We finally wandered into town and quickly found En el Camino. The albergue was heaven! We entered a courtyard surrounded by stone walls with murals on them and stone planters filled with gorgeous flowers. There was a refreshing blue pool in the middle of the courtyard and I dreamed of soaking my feet in it. The courtyard was full of luscious, green grass! I longed to take my shoes off and wander barefoot in the grass! How I had missed grass in all this landscape of rocks and dirt! It was truly an oasis after our hot, dry walk that afternoon.

When we arrived, they immediately showed us our bunks. They told us to get settled and then check in and pay later. How nice! Usually, they made us pay up front before even letting us see our beds for the night.

We got settled, took showers, and then checked in. The area where you checked in was also a bar/restaurant with nice outdoor seating under shade trees. When we finally got the waiter's attention, we both ordered a large beer and enjoyed the outdoor café. We noticed the tree above us was full of green apples and it was tempting to want to snag one off the tree but it was too high above us.

We couldn't get the wifi to connect with the password posted in numerous places around the café so we chatted at our table and watched the people arrive. A sexy guy was sweeping near us and he came by to clean the table. He said he was here to help us so we asked for the wifi password. He brought out a piece of paper with a 20-digit password. It worked! We decided to then splurge for an ice cream. When we went inside for ice cream, the same guy took our money for it. He introduced himself as Eduardo. He ended up being our waiter for both dinner and breakfast the following morning. He certainly was a jack of all trades.

We sat on the edge of the crystal clear blue pool and the blue water reminded me of the wonderful waters in the Caribbean. We soaked our feet as we ate our ice cream. I enjoyed walking barefoot through the grass, a luxury I had missed. The terrain had been so rocky that the lush grass and beautiful garden made it look like Eden.

For dinner, we ate at the albergue and had soup, salad, meatballs, ice cream, and vino. Eduardo was our excellent and very attentive waiter. We ate with a guy from France, a girl from New Zealand, a guy from Australia, a couple from Houston, and a guy from Pakistan. It was fun to chat with such a diverse crowd. While discussing incense at the pilgrims' mass in Santiago and the reason for the incense (stinky pilgrims) the Pakistan guy said he was going to do the chicken dance at the mass to pass his smelliness around. We said we would join him in the chicken dance! What a fun dinner!

Diane made another attempt to contact the airline about her trekking poles. We had just finished talking with a young woman named Jennifer, who had done the Camino two times previously and strongly advised her to get her poles. She informed us that the terrain was only going to get worse. After the terrain we had already hiked, I was not happy to hear that it was going to be more difficult ahead.

Steps: 31,594

Janet Charbonneau

Boadilla del Camino – Villacazar de Sirga

Day 13 of 31 (September 12th):
Kilometers: 19
Miles: 11.8

We had a delightful breakfast at our albergue. I looked at the big mug in front of me with a handle that looked like a coffee cup but thought it must be for cereal since it was so big. I was wrong as I realized it was indeed a coffee cup. Eduardo brought fresh toast made from great crusty bread. Next, he brought separate carafes of coffee and hot milk, which he expertly poured into our massive cups to create large café con leches. As we were leaving, I asked to take a picture of Eduardo and he disappeared; then he came out with his hands full of toast and coffee and milk containers...and posed. What a ham!

We had a great walk beside a canal. We grabbed a quick drink in Fromista and then took the river route. It was the road less taken, like the poem by my favorite poet, Robert Frost. There were no other pilgrims along the route with us; it was just us. It was a little overgrown but a nice change of pace from where we had been walking. We couldn't see the river much but we listened to all of the lovely birds and enjoyed the trees and shade.

We took a break in Villamentaro and then walked the last part to our nightly stop. The final two miles were hot and difficult. We were happy to arrive at our hostel. We were tired of all of the alburgues and I had used some of my GoFundMe money to upgrade us to a hostel. It was 40 Euros (around $45), but to not have to share a room with others was priceless! We had a great private room with twin beds dressed in white with pink accent bedspreads while the drapes were made of the same material. It was such a cute room! We loved it! It was a luxury to have a private bathroom with a tub and to have real beds to sleep in for the night.

After a shower for me and a long bath for Diane, we went to the closest bar for Sangrias. After our drink, we went inside to see if we could order some dinner. We sat there for a bit and received no service. Then we heard about an albergue serving a pilgrim's meal, so we went there for dinner. We had a great pilgrim's meal with Diane opting for the pan-fried trout which was a very different option for the main meal.

As we walked back from dinner, we ran across a statue of a pilgrim sitting at a table with a cup in front of him, as he held his walking stick. Diane and I each took a picture of us sitting next to the statue. In my picture, I held the pilgrim's cup and walking stick. I posted it on Facebook with the caption "Got caught holding a pilgrim's drink and staff!" I got all kinds of comments on that post about holding the pilgrim's "staff." Haha!

We ran into Dorene again and she said her legs were doing better. It was nice to see her moving on to finish the Camino. As we walked back to our hostel, we found a playground. We were playing on it when Dorene came by and said we weren't going to get to Santiago by playing on the playground, no matter how good the exercise was! Ha!

Steps: 33,361

Villacazar de Sirga – Calzadilla

Day 14 of 31 (September 13th):
Kilometers: 22.5
Miles: 14.0

We stopped by the albergue again for breakfast as we headed out of town. We just had our normal breakfast, toast and orange juice for me and toast and cafe con leche for Diane, except that I also had a banana. As we came up to Carrion de los Condes, we watched the sky turn black. We knew we had rain coming in really soon and we were hoping to make it to town before it dumped on us. We managed to reach the bar in town for a cold drink and to prep for the rain. As we left town, it started to rain.

We navigated through the outskirts of town in the rain and then started our journey...through 17 kilometers of nothingness. The dirt path passed through empty fields, void of any trees. The rain let up as we left town and we passed a wonderful stand holding small plums with a sign that said they were free for us to take and enjoy. It was always a pleasant surprise to see what the locals had left for you to take along your hike.

We had two solid hours of heavy winds blowing directly in our face. It was difficult to walk as the strong winds pushed against us. There were no trees to protect us against the brutal winds. Then the last few miles it rained on us with heavy winds and heavy rain. I had tied a string around my poncho to try to keep it down in the winds but it didn't help much!

We didn't talk at all those 17 kilometers. Diane walked ahead of me as normal, so I walked by myself, trying to give myself a pep talk to get through this emptiness. This was definitely the "mind" part of the Camino. There was nothing out there, just empty fields, no trees. It was a mind game...how to keep going...why was I out there...just a complete mind game. My body was on autopilot fighting the heavy winds and rain. My mind had to convince my body to continue on; my mind had to figure out why I was out there and to convince me not to quit. There was nothing out there...NOTHING! Even if I decided to quit, I had to at least walk to the next town! We were not near a roadway and had no chance of catching a taxi. We made one stop early on at a picnic table and skipped the other stops to just get to our destination for the night.

Tears were streaming down my face as I continued on in this desolate stretch of the Camino. I was determined not to quit, but this was the hardest thing that I had ever done. While my previous adventures had been difficult, they paled in comparison to this. My mind went back to one of my coworkers who didn't think I would be able to complete the journey. I gained strength in trying to prove him wrong. I couldn't quit. I had come too far to quit. I was a stubborn Charbonneau. We were known for being stubborn. I believe I got this wonderful trait from my Mom and I pulled on that stubbornness trait to keep me plodding along in the brutal wind and rain. I was determined to finish this hike and walk all the way to Santiago!

As I plodded on, I continued to battle the desire to quit with the determination to succeed. My mind reflected back to that one lone tree that I had seen a few days earlier. I wanted to be strong like that tree. I concentrated on proving the doubters wrong. I wanted to show them that I was strong enough physically and mentally to finish this walk.

I started to rediscover the inner strength in me. I knew I had accomplished everything else in my life by just taking one step at a time, even when I had no clue how I was going to obtain my goal. I went back to one of my favorite sayings that I used when starting a project that seemed too big to accomplish and I didn't know where to start, "How do you eat an elephant?" "One bite at a time." I knew that I needed to just concentrate on the next step to continue to move forward. With my new discovery, I made another step closer to my goal, followed by another.

There appeared to be no end in sight as I concentrated on each new step. Where was this next town? How much further did we have to walk? I teetered between the desire to give up and the determination to prove that I could do this. I wanted to be strong like that tree! I again concentrated on the vision of going back to work, declaring my success on the walk, and proving to myself and to everyone else that I could do it.

Continuing to play this mental game, I kept wondering where the next town was. Why couldn't we see it yet? Then, suddenly, the road dipped down and we could see through the rain that we were very close to the next town, our destination for the night. I knew at that point that I had made it! I had successfully pulled on my inner strength to make it through that desolate walk. I was single and strong like that tree! That tree now sits on the back of this book as a symbol of my new found inner strength that resided in me all along. A reminder that I am single and strong!

When we arrived at the Hostal Camino Real, we were cold and soaking wet! We stripped off some of our wet gear and left it in the foyer as we checked in. We had a private room and were thankful that we had booked it ahead of time. After slogging through the driving rain and being soaking wet the last hour, we appreciated the comfort and privacy of the room. The gentleman running the place was extremely nice! He gave us newspapers to put into our shoes to help them dry and told us to bring our wet clothes downstairs and they would send it through the dryer.

After we settled in, we took showers and put warm, dry clothes on. We sent our clothes to be dried. We headed to the bar and I ordered a large beer. I saw that they had pizza available and it looked pretty good so I ordered that for dinner. It was delicious and a welcomed comfort food after slogging all day through the winds and the rain. We also treated ourselves to some Magnum ice cream bars as a reward for making it through a very difficult day.

We again ran into the lady from Wisconsin and two ladies from California whom we had met as we were leaving Boadilla, as well as Jennifer who we met at the Boadilla hostel and the young guy who plays guitar that we met in Hornillos del Camino. They were all staying in the adjoining albergue.

We found out that our friend Dorene had gone home. Her legs were good, but she ended up with stomach issues. We were sorry to hear that she had given up! This was her second attempt to finish the Camino, so I know she hated to quit again. I can't imagine not reaching Santiago. I wonder if it is easier when you are a short plane ride away from another attempt. It was an expensive plane ticket if I had to make a second attempt, so I was strongly determined to reach Santiago on my first try. Even the excruciating knee pain was not going to stop me from reaching my destination!

While we already had many difficult days physically, I believe this one was the hardest so far since it was difficult both physically and mentally. Thankfully it was flat terrain, so it was not hard on my knees, but the relentless winds and rain made it very laborious to walk. Then the long stretch of nothingness with no towns to break up the hike was extremely challenging. Happily, we were finished with another tough day and still going strong ready for the next day!

Steps: 31,375

Janet Charbonneau

Calzadilla – Sahagun

Day 15 of 31 (September 14th):
Kilometers: 22.4
Miles: 14.0

We had an excellent buffet breakfast at the hostel. It was such a treat for us. I had scrambled eggs with ham, toast, juice, and coffee. It was so rare to get eggs for breakfast that I really enjoyed them!

I didn't have much energy in the first couple of hours. It was extremely hard to continue to walk! I was happy that the terrain was still flat. The wind was blowing 25-30 mph in our face, but at least it was sunny! Thankfully, there were many towns along the way to break up the walk. As we wandered through one of the small towns, we came to an intersection in the road which had yellow arrows pointing in two different directions. As Diane stated later, we just had to play rock, paper, scissors to see which one of us would make the call and decide a direction. We lucked out and found another Camino arrow further on.

We passed a sweet looking dog that looked like he was a German Shepherd mix. He was lying down and intently staring at a set of glass doors a few feet away, obviously waiting for his owner to come out of the restaurant. He was so cute! It brought up the desire to have a dog again.

The Journey Inward

In one of the cafés, we ran into the Wisconsin woman with the California girls. We started walking with those three ladies as we approached Moratino. The terrain had been pretty flat but we saw a large hill up ahead with doors on the sides of the hill. Diane said they looked like Hobbit houses and wouldn't you know the sign that provided some background said: "No, these are not Hobbit houses." They were bodegas which were caves that were used in the past for food storage and wine-making. Each doorway was surrounded by brick and concrete entrances.

The surrounding fields used to be full of grapes and the bodegas were full of wine-presses, barrels, massive clay vessels and bottling vats. This is where they used to make their own wines each year. Too bad they weren't still full of wine! They are still sometimes used to store cheese, hams, and vegetables. The sign said they were probably at least 500 years old.

At one point we crossed the street and continued on a path similar to the one we had been walking on. Up high on a mountain, a man yelled at us and he motioned for us to go the other way. We hesitated, turned around momentarily, but then turned and continued on in our original direction, since we thought we were going the right direction and wasn't sure why he was yelling. He yelled again. We did this a couple times and he yelled at us every time we tried to go the wrong way. We even had another pilgrim join us and he too had gone along our route. All three of us finally turned back to the road and found the correct route. We had missed an arrow showing a left turn and an "X" on the back of a stop sign showing that we should not have gone straight. Our Camino angel saved us!

We finally made it to Sahagun and ran into Jennifer at an outside bar. We were trying to find a place to stay so we continued on. We were looking a bit lost, not sure if we were on the right track when Lennart walked out of an albergue right in front of us. You again!! Haha! He said it was a nice place and we ended up staying there. The funny thing was that we were looking for that albergue and would have missed it if Lennart had not walked out. He was our second Camino angel!!

After showers and hanging up our wet clothes to dry, we headed back to town to find an ATM and a bar. We found an ATM and then as we were passing a café, we saw a playground. It had a red parrot that rocked back and forth on a spring. Since I used to live on a sailboat and was a big Jimmy Buffett fan (a definite Parrothead), it just seemed to fit my personality, so I had to attempt to ride it. I barely fit into the seat. The parrot ride was really springy so I had to hold on tightly hoping I would not fall out of it onto the ground. I asked Diane to take a picture of me being a kid again on the playground; we had to have some fun along the way!

We continued on and found an Irish pub where we stopped and each of us had a coffee with Baileys to warm us up. The Swedish couple was planning on eating dinner at the Irish bar, but they ended up changing their mind and ate at the albergue.

We had a great pilgrim meal with our Swedish couple along with the girl from Taiwan, a Czech guy, and the German mother and daughter (Click n Clack) that we had seen and heard so many days along the trail. We had to laugh because we were in a monastery again and we had to be quiet since nuns were above us on the next floor. We kept getting shushed by the staff. The meal was filling but there weren't any choices; everybody got the same thing. At least there was wine!

There were four beds in the room we were staying in and we had met the other couple who would be sharing our room with us before we went to dinner. They were a couple from Ireland who were not really a couple but were just two friends who had decided to hike together. We knew they were going to go out to dinner and would be coming in later so we got to enjoy the peace and quiet for a while.

While getting ready for bed, I brushed my teeth and was taken aback by a loud click! I realized my toothbrush broke! I had to finish brushing my teeth with a two-inch toothbrush and figured I would

The Journey Inward

have to probably wait until Leon to be able to purchase a new one. Oh well, at least it was slightly usable until then.

I posted a picture from the day on Facebook where we ran across a place where there were arrows pointing in two directions at an intersection. I questioned which direction to go and Diane commented on the post that "Most of the time we just wing it. ...or if we disagree, we play rock, paper, scissors. Janet cheats." My response was "That's because I was playing Rock Paper Scissors Lizard Spock. Haha!" It was in the realm of "The Big Bang Theory". The humor on our posts helped get us through the reality of the number of days we still had left to hike.

Since we were almost halfway to Santiago, when I pulled my journal out I realized that I wouldn't even fill half of it. I should have gotten a lighter journal with fewer pages. I pulled out about a third of the pages at the end and threw them away. I was still working on having less weight in my backpack.

I crawled into bed and wrote in my journal. The room was very cold! I wondered if all the rooms were this cold or if it was because we were at the end of the building. I pulled out my small flannel blanket and huddled under it as I finally fell asleep.

Steps: 36,932

Sahagun – Reliegos

Day 16 of 31 (September 15th):
Kilometers: 31.2
Miles: 19.4

Breakfast was only served between 6:30 and 7:00 a.m. at the albergue. We were served a cup of coffee and two very small muffins. It was an extremely grim breakfast! Our friend was refused when he asked for another cup of coffee. We should have found breakfast elsewhere. After a couple of hours walking, we stopped in Bercianos del Camino and Diane ordered a bocadillo that was huge! She shared some of it with me and it was really good.

We stopped at a bar in El Burgo Ranero for a drink and the owner showed off his homemade vegetable soup. I am usually not a soup person but my throat hurt and I just couldn't resist it. It had noodles and vegetables in a chicken broth and it was fantastic! That really says a lot since I never get excited over soup! As we were getting ready to leave, we saw our Swedish couple stick their heads in the bar. They were staying in that town for the night, so I highly recommended their soup.

We had a long slog to our town and spent the last two hours in the rain. It seemed to be a never-ending trek. Where was this town? My left calf started to get a searing pain inside and it ended up feeling like a charley horse cramp. I limped into town. We trudged all the way through town and couldn't find our hostel, La Parada. Miserable, we turned around and plodded back through town, desperate to find our hostel for the night! We asked for directions twice and finally found it.

We again had chosen a private room and it was on the first floor away from the other rooms which were on the second floor. The rooms near us were not occupied, so the shared bathroom ended up being a private bathroom. After showers, I gave Diane money to help with the washer and dryer cost and she went to go wash our clothes. The washing machine said 4 Euros and Diane put in 4 Euros and it still would not start. Then the manager came out and said she needed a token. He made her pay 4 Euros for the token and would not acknowledge that she had already put in 4 Euros already! She got tired of arguing with him and decided to sacrifice the extra 4 Euros. Not very good hospitality!!

We were both so glad to finally be dry and warm and to be able to actually wash our laundry in a machine and dry it. The dining area was across the hall and there was a large group of men playing a card game that we had seen being played in other places. They were loud and kept slamming their hands on the table. Whatever it was, they were having lots of fun!

We had a very nice pilgrim's dinner at the hostel and met Paul and Jeanne from the west coast of the United States. Jeanne and I ordered the soup as our first course. They put the entire pot of soup on the table for us and we were able to help ourselves to seconds. After being cold and not feeling well, the soup was a welcome first course. We stuffed our boots with newspapers again hoping they would dry out by morning. The room was quiet, warm, and dry, and that was all we could hope for. We had crossed our halfway point during the day and it was rewarding to have achieved that accomplishment. I was proud to have made it this far. With the Tiger Balm helping my knees each night, I was feeling pretty confident that I was actually going to be able to complete the walk!

Janet Charbonneau

Steps: 40,777

Reliegos – Leon

Day 17 of 31 (September 16th):
Kilometers: 23.9
Miles: 14.9

We left La Parada and wandered around Reliegos looking for a place for breakfast. Frustrated after zigzagging through town with no luck, we found our way back to the Camino route and wandered out of town. As we walked onto the outskirts of town, we ran across a wonderful stand with three boxes of small plums. There was a sign that said they were free and to please take some so we did! The Spanish hospitality was always so amazing!

We decided that we would walk to Mansilla de las Mulas and then catch a bus to Leon. Both of our guidebooks recommended this and one of them gave a very long explanation of why you should consider the bus and why you should not feel obligated to walk the entire way, convincing you that it is your Camino and you can take a bus when you decide it is necessary. One of the guidebooks said to "be on alert for trail markers, detours, and traffic." The trail runs next to a busy road and through a highly industrial area. We decided to take the guidebook's advice. After the horrible slog through Villafria on the outskirts of Burgos, we decided that it was safer to take a bus for 10 kilometers and bypass that industrial trek into Leon.

The storm clouds started moving in as we walked along the desolate route to Mansilla de las Mulas. This route offered very little in the way of beauty. The path was right next to the long, straight, flat road.

Diane finally stopped and said she wanted to get her rain gear on. She just felt it was coming soon. It took me a few minutes to get my poncho set up again over my backpack, but Diane was right and the rains came in. Not only did the rains come in but the predicted winds came with it!

As the winds increased, I became more and more enraged with fighting with my poncho. The winds picked up to 25-35 mph and were very consistent. To make it worse, they were blowing from the side. I tried to hold my poncho down, but how do you hold it in place when the winds are strongly blowing from the side? The rain poured down and then the winds increased! There was nothing around for protection, just flat land for many miles and a perfect platform for the wind to come blasting past us! This was turning into a very nasty storm. The winds increased to 40 mph gusts and then just blew a consistent 40 mph.

I was doing my best to stay upright as the strong winds threatened to knock me over. I tried to tame my poncho but in those winds, I was completely helpless! Honestly, that poncho was blowing all over the place, so I was quite the sight! I was getting frustrated from the battle. I eventually just stopped, took a deep breath and laughed at myself! I could see myself from an outsider's view and knew I looked ridiculous. There was no use in getting flustered with the situation, so all I could do was laugh!

Diane told me later that day that when she had looked back to make sure I was still there that all she could see was the poncho blowing up over my head; she believed I was somewhere underneath it!

Thankfully, the rain did not last very long but the winds never let up at all. Since I had such a hard time fighting with my poncho, I had slowed down and Diane was quite a distance ahead of me. I did see

The Journey Inward

a taxi drive by but didn't see it until it passed me. As frustrated as I was with the winds, rain, and poncho, if I had seen it sooner, I would have flagged it down and had him take us to Leon. I would have said, "Let's forget the walk and the bus!" I continued to slog further and also continued to fight with my poncho. The winds subsided a bit but were still blowing 25-35 mph. I finally just gave up on my poncho. The sky looked like it had cleared and I was beyond done with fighting the poncho, so I stripped it off and rolled it into a ball. I held it with one hand while I continued to use my trekking poles to assist my journey. I had to take a deep breath and just go with the flow. I was way behind Diane, but I chalked it up to my fight with Mother Nature. I again attempted to work on my patience and be happy with where I was.

The trip was only 10 kilometers, but it was feeling like a lot longer than that! Literally, that was only about six miles, which was nothing compared to what we were used to walking. I guess I was just fed up with the fight with the winds and the poncho; the walk stretched on. It seemed to last forever! We finally approached Mansilla de las Mulas and walked into town. We followed the signs towards the bus station and found a café that was open. Diane got her usual café con leche while I ordered an Aquarius. I also wanted some Vitamin C and was glad that orange juice was available, so I ordered that as well. Unfortunately, it was bottled and not fresh squeezed. I was disappointed as I had become accustomed to freshly squeezed juice. We both ordered a Bocadillo since we were hungry after having had no breakfast.

It was a very comfortable café and we enjoyed watching the normal everyday routines where the various vendors were bringing their breads and wares to sell to the café owner. It was so different from our restaurants in the United States.

We finished our lunch and wandered out to locate the bus station. It didn't take us long to find the path to the station and we wandered in to find our bus. We found that we had a 30-minute wait and that you just paid on the bus directly to the driver. We put our packs down and waited near the area where the bus would arrive.

Our bus arrived and we prepared to board. The driver indicated that we had to put our backpacks in the cargo area of the bus; we could not bring them on board. He was courteous enough to help us load the packs. He then boarded the bus and let us come on and pay him directly. Holy smokes, he was a cutie! We had an enjoyable trip to Leon with a sweet view of our sexy bus driver the entire way. Spain is quite nice!

We watched the sights out of the bus windows as we headed into Leon. We saw some pilgrims walking into Leon, but we didn't feel bad about taking the bus through this area. We got into the bus station and navigated to a door leading to the streets of Leon. We stopped to look at the map and figure out what part of town we were in, and how to get to the hostel for the evening. We exited, turned left, and looked for a street that crossed the river into Leon. Once we crossed the river, we again referenced the map to check where we were and continued to walk towards our destination.

I saw a Pharmacia and told Diane that I wanted to stop and look for a toothbrush to replace my broken one. I managed to find a sturdy, folding travel toothbrush and bought some more toothpaste to go with it. I also found some throat lozenges to help my sore throat.

We continued to walk through Leon and towards the Cathedral since we knew our hostel was nearby. As we came close to the cathedral, we looked up towards an outdoor café and guess who was sitting at an outside table drinking wine? It was our favorite Swedish couple! As we spotted them, Lennart stood up and loudly yelled, "The Americans are here!" We excitedly walked over to them and we all hugged each other. What are the odds of wandering through this huge city and running into our Swedish friends again? It was a special type of Camino magic where we amazingly ran into people along the way at just the right time.

After catching up with them for a while, we headed back out to search for our hostel. We realized we had walked too far, so we had to turn around. Hmm, if we had not missed our turn then we would not have run into our Swedish friends. How interesting to see our mistake was our good fortune!

We finally got to the street where our hostel was, but after wandering back and forth on that street we couldn't find it! On our third trip, I finally noticed the blue "H" representing Hostel, so I knew we were close; it was so close that it would have bitten us! We finally noticed a tiny sign with the name of the Hostel, San Martin, above a door. We walked in the door and wandered around and still couldn't find it. We walked up two flights of stairs and finally found the entrance door! Good grief, how difficult could they make it? We were early but they said our room was ready so they checked us in; then Diane was presented with a gift: her package from Air France!! She finally received her trekking poles and toiletries! It was received 17 days after starting our journey! Diane was thrilled to be reunited with her toiletries and looked forward to finally being able to use her trekking poles, especially with the mountains ahead of us.

Our room was fairly nice, with a tub in the bathroom and working internet! Since there was a tub, I told Diane to enjoy the tub while I checked in on Facebook and caught up with family and friends back home.

Once our bathing and clothes washing routines were complete, we headed out to explore. We stopped by the Museo de San Isidoro and toured it. While all of the artifacts were interesting, I fell in love with the huge library filled with ancient books! I wished I could have actually explored them, but since we couldn't touch them I just had to marvel at the thought of what was in all these books.

We kept our eyes on the stores we passed hoping to find a place where we could purchase a fleece jacket, but never found a store that looked like it would sell them. We went in search of a place where we could find replacement pilgrim passports since ours were rapidly filling up with stamps. We already had 34 stamps and were down to our last page. We ran into our Swedish friends again and they assisted us with our search. We tried to find the Asociacion de Amigos del

Camino where the guidebook said we could get another credential, but never found it after several attempts. We found the Tourism Office, but they didn't have any. They directed us to a nearby hostel which ended up being a youth hostel with nobody inside that could help us. We gave up and decided to try at our next night's albergue.

It was that time of day again where it would have been dinnertime at home, but most of the restaurants were closed until later in the evening. We aimlessly strolled from restaurant to restaurant looking at menus (the majority of them were in Spanish only) and the times that they opened for dinner. We were frustrated to see that almost all of them opened at 8:00 p.m. and were expensive. After much wandering on the streets we decided to head into a quaint little wine bar for a glass of wine and a chance to warm up and relax. Along with our glasses of wine, we were handed a bowl of munchies which included nuts, some other crunchy items, and gummy bears! What a very strange combination! I am not sure who thought that made up a nice combo? After trying the very, very hard and chewy gummy bears, we stuck with the other salty items in the bowl, leaving a pool of gummies at the bottom of the bowl when we left.

We wandered back to a little dive restaurant that promised a pilgrim's meal and we didn't have to wait until 8 pm for it. As our usual wine came to our table it was presented in a most unusual way. It came in a bottle which looked like an olive oil bottle which we would realize later was actually a liquor bottle from one of their locally made liquors. And the glasses were not wine glasses but, instead, were Amstel beer glasses! Oh well, it still tasted like red wine, so we drank it as we nibbled on the tasty crusty bread that was brought with it.

I was tired of the usual first courses, so I decided to try the pasta as a first course this time. As expected it was very filling and I had eaten less than half when our second course came out. I gave up on the pasta and proceeded with my chicken and fries, along with my wine in a beer glass. We finished our meal and stepped out into the cold weather, hurrying back through the winding route to our hotel.

The Journey Inward

As I cuddled in my bed, I was happy to finally have some good internet to be able to continue with my online journal.

Steps: 22,544

Leon – San Martin del Camino

Day 18 of 31 (September 17th):
Kilometers: 25.4
Miles: 15.8

We wandered through the streets of Leon beginning our journey for the day. One of the Camino markers showed that we had 306 kilometers left to reach Santiago, which is just over 190 miles. It sounded like a lot of kilometers left to walk, but we had walked more than that already, so we knew we could do it.

We found an open café and stopped for breakfast. As we left the breakfast shop, Diane went searching for her glasses and couldn't find them. She headed back into the café and thankfully found them near our table on the floor! That was a close one!

We continued to peer into store windows looking for a nice fleece jacket or sweatshirt to keep us warmer than our current layers. We were tired of the cold mornings! Having no luck, we tromped on.

We ran across the magnificent, ornate Parador de San Marcos hotel where the characters in the movie, *The Way*, stopped. It was an extremely extravagant hotel and, had I realized that it was in Leon, I believe I would have splurged and stayed there. It would have been worth it! I was disappointed and kicking myself because I had missed the opportunity to stay there. This is where I needed to calm my mind and say it was OK for not being prepared and knowing everything ahead of time. I needed to just take it one day at a time and see what life brought me. It was a reminder to just let it go and relax.

In front of the hotel, there was a statue of a pilgrim sitting on some steps and resting his head back on a pillar; his shoes rested beside his tired feet. He seemed at peace and I needed to be at peace as well and not frustrated at lost opportunities.

It was a very long walk just to get out of Leon! The city streets just kept on going and when we would turn a corner we would see more city streets to walk. We stopped for a break and to get something to drink. We finally started exiting the suburbs of Leon and came across a small table with a box of plums on it. A stamp and ink pad sat next to it. There was a basket hanging nearby with cookies in it and a bench on the other side for resting. We passed by it and then were stopped by an elderly gentleman who turned us around and told us to get a cookie and some plums. We were grateful for the stop and it allowed me to get to my fanny pack in order to get my ibuprofen which I needed to take for my knee. I had continued to take ibuprofen along with using the Tiger Balm and it seemed to be working well for me.

The gentleman handed both of us two plums and a cookie, motioned to us that there was also a stamp available for our Camino passport, and asked us to sign his guestbook. The stamp said "Un amigo del Camino y del Peregrino te desea mucha suerte en el Camino" which meant that he is a friend of the Camino and pilgrims and wished us good luck along the way. It was a very surprising and pleasant stop from our gracious host! These moments are what made the walk so special!

The walk was fairly pleasant along a trail next to the highway. We ran across a cute little white kitten and stopped to pet him. As we were petting the kitten one of the bikers stopped along with us. He joked and said, "I believe the cat's name is Stevens," so Diane and I chuckled at the reference to the singer-songwriter, Cat Stevens. It helps to have a little humor to make your walk go by faster and we were grateful for his lame attempt at humor!

We finally approached San Martin del Camino and found our albergue, Vieira. It was a quaint family run place and they were very welcoming! As they stamped our passports, we asked if they had passports available. They did have them for sale and we both purchased one since we only had room for 3 more stamps in our current passports. After getting settled in and a shower, we went for a drink and they included tapas along with our drink. Since we finished early and dinner was a ways away, we opted to have a couple of drinks and they included something extra with each one. We were very grateful for having something to nibble on before our group dinner.

The albergue had some cool mementos in their cabinet for sale, so I bought a couple of magnets to remember the journey. One of them was for a friend of mine back home. The magnet showed a pilgrim and the starburst shell symbol of the Camino, so I thought it was a perfect reminder of the journey.

Dinner time finally came and we were served a tasty squash soup with squash from their garden! Our second course was a savory chicken with potatoes. It was a wonderful homemade meal and it was greatly appreciated! We met a young girl from Spain who had just started her Camino that day. The rest of the table spoke French and we could not understand them, so we spent our meal working with the limited English from our new Spanish friend.

After dinner, we attempted to go to sleep early but were rudely interrupted by the constant talk from the French group who shared our room. Finally, they wound down and went to sleep, so the rest of the room could sleep as well.

Steps: 30,384

San Martin del Camino – San Justo

Day 19 of 31 (September 18th):
Kilometers: 20.9
Miles: 13.0

I woke up with the date seared in my brain. It was my brother Den's birthday. The only problem was that I couldn't text him a Happy Birthday. I had lost him two years prior in a freak motorcycle accident when a deer sideswiped him on his motorcycle and he died on the spot. I missed him tremendously. I lay in bed in tears, quietly sobbing as I laid there thinking of him.

While he had been 18 years older than me, I got a chance to really get to know him when I was in my 30's as Blaine and I went to visit him and my sister-in-law every year. My family was a close family and I was finally able to be close to my brother. I loved him dearly and loved the times that I got to spend with him. He had always been so vibrant and full of life but in a quiet, laid-back sort of way. Like my other brother, he knew how to live life to the fullest. He was kind and would always lend a helping hand to someone in need. Thinking back on the day I lost him, I lay there remembering the shock of the loss.

I was an emotional mess and didn't know how I was going to get the strength to walk for the day.

As I got dressed for the day, I vowed to walk in his memory for the day. He had inspired me to live life to the fullest and he would have loved to have followed my journey across northern Spain. I knew his spirit was with me that day.

We prepared to leave and I purchased an Aquarius before we left the albergue. Our gracious host hugged us and gave each of us a package which contained a hat and a badge holder lanyard. They were very appreciative to have us stay there. We loved their hospitality! We had wonderful experiences in family-owned albergues.

We walked out of the albergue and immediately bundled up on extra layers! It was 39 degrees outside and one of our coldest mornings yet! Neither of us was prepared for this type of weather. Actually, we had discussed the weather a couple of days before we left and saw that the forecast was for colder weather than we had planned. Therefore, both of us threw in an extra layer at the last minute. My extra layer consisted of wind-proof leggings I had used on our Harley trip along with a long sleeve Under Armour shirt which was a thin layer but warm and easy to wash and dry. I also used my extremely thin Columbia sun shirt as a middle layer and it worked amazingly well to keep me insulated and warm. I had my blue workout jacket on top. I used my sarong as a scarf and it was perfect! I never thought I would end up using it as a scarf. With all the extra layers, it was still cold, but bearable to walk.

While the Tiger Balm had been helping my knees be pain-free each morning, the cold was making them painful again. They felt very stiff. I hoped that when it finally warmed up for the day that they would start to feel better.

As we started walking, I was grateful that I had brought the wind-resistant pants. While wearing them, I was reminded of our Harley trip. Den was the reason we took the Harley trip. After not having a motorcycle since he was in his twenties, at age 56 he bought a new Harley. While Blaine and I were out visiting him and my sister-in-law, Debbie, he took me for a ride on the bike. I loved it and the idea of riding across the country on a motorcycle became our discussion that evening over dinner. I smiled at the memory of that discussion and the Harley trip that came as a result of that discussion. Den had been the spark that started the ball rolling. The memory turned bittersweet as the pain of his loss hit me again. I felt the heat of the tears against my cheeks once again as they rolled down them. I swiped them away as I walked along knowing that my brother was guiding me that day. I knew his spirit was with me and he would want me laughing, not crying.

We had a beautiful scenic walk along a dirt path covered with shade trees which paralleled the road and it was very enjoyable! As the day warmed up, we started to strip our layers. My knees were starting to feel better as the cold dissipated into the warm day.

We stopped for a snack at the Bar El Puente outside of Hospital de Orbigo. It was a very nice bar with great inside seating. I ordered a fresh squeezed orange juice and it was served in a wine glass. I was becoming very spoiled with all the fresh squeezed orange juice.

The bathroom was huge and luxurious like it belonged in an expensive hotel, very different than our normal stops! They had a beautiful courtyard in the back containing wonderful flowers along with cockatiels and various other birds in cages. They had fragrant roses and I walked across the luscious green grass to smell them. You must take time to smell the roses! Their aroma was an exquisitely sweet smell which was such a joy. We enjoyed relaxing and wandering in the peaceful setting before continuing on our journey.

As we walked on, we came upon a magnificent medieval bridge over a beautiful river. While the river was not that wide (there were only about three arches that were over the actual river), the bridge stretched over nineteen arches into the town of Hospital de Orbigo. The legend says that there was a knight, Don Suero de Quinones, from Leon who was rejected by the lady he loved. In order to break the bonds of this love, he decided to wear an iron collar and declared that he would defeat 300 knights to gain his honor back. After breaking 200 lances he was declared successful. He removed his collar and proceeded on a pilgrimage to Santiago, finally freed from his bonds of love.

The river was a very pleasant sight and I enjoyed walking over the stone bridge. We passed through Hospital de Orbigo and continued on as the flatness of the Meseta finally gave way to rolling hills. While I did enjoy having flat terrain for walking, I had to admit I was happy to see some hills. It was a sign that the "mind" part of the Camino was ending and the "soul" part was coming up. I was curious to see what this last section would bring. I was joyful to have made it through the boring Meseta and to be entering the mountains again. It was much more interesting terrain to pass through! We passed a field full of round bales of hay and continued up into the hills. We passed a weird plant with spiky green pods that looked like they turned brown and split open to release whatever they held. We couldn't figure out what they were or what they held. Later research showed that it was probably datura or jimsonweed.

We came across a statue which was dressed in clothing. From earlier pilgrims, I had heard about this statue. It seems to have different clothes on as the years go by. He looked like a stone statue but had skeleton-like hands sticking out of his coat. Today it was dressed in green pants with a smiley face drawn on them. He wore a medium length purple coat, purple headband, and tennis shoes. He stood next to a large pile of rocks and a stone cross. We had no idea why he was there!

We continued to walk up a hill and guess who we ran into again? The Swedish couple we adored! We thought they were a day or two ahead of us, so were pleasantly surprised to run into them again and chat with them for a bit. At our fast pace, we passed them and eventually approached a well-known refreshment stand with a spiral of rocks that can be seen as you approach it. A gentleman named David runs this small stand in the middle of nowhere about 3 kilometers from the next town. He provides fresh fruit and juices to the pilgrims passing by. He has a donation jar but doesn't expect you to pay for what you take. The donations are for providing for the next pilgrim. The sign on the cart translates to "The key to the essence is the presence." He lives there with no running water or electricity. It is a very welcoming rest spot. The Swedes caught up with us and we chatted a few more minutes as we enjoyed the rest stop. Then we continued on knowing our beloved Swedes would pass us to stay in Astorga for the night.

We walked through orchards as we looked at the mountains in the distance and then came upon a stone cross just before our stop for the night. We saw Astorga in the distance and then ran across a fountain with a large statue next to it of a pilgrim drinking water. Since we were just outside of our stop for the day, we skipped the fountain and headed into town. We had originally planned to stay in Astorga, but when we tried to book a reservation there, everything was full. We thought that it might still be full of news media attempting to follow-up on the news of a body found, which ended up being that of a pilgrim who went missing in April. She was last seen in Astorga on April 5th and her killer and body were finally found on September 11th. Astorga had been full of news media covering the story since then.

We had known of the missing pilgrim before we headed out on our journey, so we made sure we stayed together, were aware of our surroundings, and stayed on the trail. We hadn't told any of our friends or relatives because we both knew the Camino was safe to hike and we didn't want anyone worrying about our safety.

It was still chilling to find out that the killer had probably lured her via false yellow arrows onto his property, where he killed her. This was another reminder of how truly short life really is. It came full circle with the thoughts from the morning. It was my brother's birthday and he passed away too soon. I had lost my other brother, Paul, when I was just 23 and he was just short of turning 34. He died suddenly of an aneurysm. After losing both brothers and my father, this reminder of unexpected death was very close to my heart. It bore into me the idea that we should live every day to the fullest and hike your Camino while you still can! It was a reminder to take chances while I still could. I was very grateful to be able to walk the Camino, meet such wonderful people, and enjoy this unique experience.

As we wandered into town, it didn't take very long to find our hostel, Hostal Juli, for the night, especially since it wasn't a big town. We looked forward to our private room after sharing our room with eight other people the previous night. We especially appreciated the private bathroom! We checked in and found out that they would do laundry for us, so we quickly took showers and brought our laundry to them. Our room also had a balcony with a couple of chairs. It was such a treat to sit on the balcony and watch the world go by. We watched a few cats wandering around in the courtyard below.

We went to the bar for a glass of sangria and they didn't have it, so we tried our first Tinto de Verano, which is essentially red wine with a lemon-lime drink mixed with it. It was really refreshing! It was our new favorite if Sangria wasn't an option! The bartender gave us a bowl of olives along with our drinks and we wandered outside for some sunshine and to relax for a while. Since I don't like olives, I got hungry and decided to buy some chips at the bar, which was a splurge since I never eat chips. My bag of chips was served on a plate! Haha! We sat there enjoying our sunshine and another round of drinks. It was a pleasure after having completed our miles for the day.

I had noticed a Pharmacia resided across the street from the hostel when we arrived, but it was closed for their midday break. When it opened, I headed across the street to find something for my stuffy sinuses. As luck would have it, the pharmacist didn't speak English. After a great effort of asking for pseudoephedrine and a charades game of symptoms, he finally brought me back around his counter over to his computer so I could type in my symptoms into a translator! I finally was handed a nasal spray with a charades game of how often to use it. It was times like this that I wished I had learned more Spanish. While most of the time we could cope with the hindrance, it would have been very beneficial to know more Spanish to talk to the pharmacist and to be able to talk to everyone when we were making reservations for our next place to stay!

The Journey Inward

When I returned, I was excited to see that dinner was finally being served! We had been patiently waiting for the pilgrim's menu to become available. I have never been a big fan of soups, but after the cold weather and with my stuffy nose, I craved the soup when it was an option on the pilgrim's menu for the first course. It was a wonderful chicken broth with noodles and, when they brought out soup, they brought out a whole pot of it, even if just for one person! I devoured two bowls of it and it made me feel so much better! I enjoyed my second course as well, but the soup was such a comfort food! After a nice dinner, we wandered up to our room to enjoy the peace and quiet of our private room.

Steps: 29,772

Janet Charbonneau

San Justo – Rabanal

Day 20 of 31 (September 19th):
Kilometers: 23.3
Miles: 14.5

We started our day with a little breakfast at the hostel and I enjoyed a fresh squeezed orange juice with the juice of three oranges. We stepped out into a brutally cold morning. As we headed into the town, we crossed a maze of green metal steps and ramps to get us safely over some train tracks. It was a short walk into Astorga and we got there so early that everything was still closed, so we found no chocolate and no warm clothes! We were disappointed since the town is known for their chocolate, but no stores were open for us to buy any of it. As we wandered through the town, we finally found an ATM.

On our way up to it, we noticed a pilgrim's passport on the ground. Diane picked it up and saw that it belonged to a Canadian pilgrim. We went in to get money from the ATM as we discussed our best options to try to locate the missing pilgrim. As we left the ATM, still discussing our options, we found a couple wandering around looking at the ground. We asked if they had lost a passport and they were the ones! They introduced themselves as Hugh and Nancy and they were ecstatic to have found the passport. They were very worried to travel ahead without it, get to the next albergue, and be turned away since he didn't have his pilgrim's passport. The passport was required in order to stay at any of the pilgrim albergues. They had spent the past hour retracing all of their steps, too afraid to wander ahead and be denied a place to stay. We definitely made their day!

We continued through Astorga desperately looking for a store selling warm clothes, but nothing was open in the entire town. We didn't want to delay our hike so we plodded on. We came upon the Palacio de Gaudi which was a palace for Archbishop Juan Bautista Grau Villespinos. It reminded me of a palace out of Disney World! Next to it stood a beautiful cathedral with ornate figures sculpted all over it. After taking many pictures of these two remarkable buildings, we headed out of town.

A short while later, we were walking along the highway when we saw a gentleman off to our right side who appeared to be raking through the dirt piles, a farmer working on his land. We watched him as he worked. He stopped what he was doing when he spotted us. He then raised his hands and arms overhead back and then towards our route, back and forth, and yelled "Buen Camino!" We yelled a surprised "Thank you" back to him with huge grins on our faces. It was so special to get the encouragement when you least expected it. The people along the Camino are so awesome and inspiring!

By the time we arrived in Murias, it was a good time for a mid-morning break and my refreshing Aquarius. We found a little spot called Meson el Llar that looked like it would be a good resting spot. We put our stuff down at a table out front and stepped in to find a drink and possibly a snack. The lady who owned the place was behind the counter and, when asked for an Aquarius, she stated that she only carried homemade drinks...smoothies. So I stepped out of my comfort zone and ordered one of her smoothies. As she made it, she talked about some of the ingredients going into it: celery, fennel, ginger, and who knows what else ended up in there. I was handed a pea green smoothie and I just hoped that all those fresh ingredients would help kick that cold out of me! I picked up a banana and a couple of nut bars, paid for everything, and headed back out to grab a seat and sip my mysterious smoothie. As I added a tip to her tip jar, she said all the tips "go to the dogs." That was cool! I was happy to be helping the canine population with their special treats!

My honest opinion of my smoothie was that it was okay; the ginger was good in it. I can't say it was as refreshing as I was hoping for in a mid-morning break drink but I hoped the natural ingredients would help me with my cold. I sat there drinking my smoothie and enjoying the beautiful red, pink and white flowers that were overflowing the flower boxes just below each window on the building next door.

Diane came out with her refreshments and joined me at the table. We started talking about reaching Cruz de Ferro the following day. It is a tradition to carry a stone with you the entire Camino and then to toss that stone at Cruz de Ferro. It symbolizes tossing out all of your burdens and continuing on with the weight of the world finally off of you!

Diane told me that she had been carrying four stones to leave at Cruz de Ferro. She told me that one of them was grey with lines of white. It represented her family ties that bound her. She said that she found herself to be the rock for everyone and it was weighing on her. Being there to always help her siblings and aging parents was taking a toll on her. She said she needed to learn to take care of herself and to know it was alright to say no occasionally.

One of her other rocks was pink and it represented her heart, broken and bruised, fragile yet guarded. She said that she needed to forgive herself for believing that she was not good enough. I knew how she felt. I often had the same feelings. I stayed in my last relationship way too long, allowing him to control the relationship and to see me when it was convenient for him. I guess I felt grateful to finally be back in a relationship; therefore, I didn't take a stand when he stood me up or changed plans at the last minute. I was thankful that he hit my last nerve when he stood me up on my 50th birthday and I broke off the relationship. I was proud of myself for finally standing up for myself. Like Diane, I needed to realize that I was good enough and I deserved to be treated right by a man.

The Journey Inward

I told Diane about my stone. Actually, it really wasn't a stone; it was a sea heart which was a seed that falls from a vine and can float off in the ocean to drift to different countries until it washes up on a beach somewhere. It had the appearance of dark brown wood and it was in the shape of a heart. I had found it on a deserted beach in the Bahamas while we were cruising. Like the sea heart, I felt that I had been drifting through life lately with no direction. I felt the sea heart represented my broken heart, my failed marriage, and the mound of debt from the failed business. I needed to quit blaming myself for getting into this predicament and feeling like a failure. I needed to also quit being so guarded and let my heart open up again. I was looking forward to releasing these burdens!

At our next stop, it was finally warm enough to strip a layer. Since my bottom layer was the wind resistance leggings, I had to stop at a place where I could switch them for shorts. We found another bar to rest and buy a drink. I ran in and switched my warm leggings for shorts. I found a cute mannequin of a pilgrim gentleman with long gray hair and a mustache. He wore a shell around his neck and a shell on the inside brim of his dark brown hat, which was folded straight up to be visible. He carried a walking staff. I asked Diane to take a picture of me and this pilgrim.

We continued and came to a wire fence with hundreds of crosses attached to it. They were all made of sticks of various sizes and held together in many different ways; many were attached with colorful ribbon. I was curious to know the background of all these unique crosses. What burdens did these crosses bear of previous pilgrims? Did leaving the cross alleviate any pain and suffering?

We continued on and finally entered the town of Rabanal. We had a reservation at the albergue, so we found our spot for the night and went to check in. The guy who checked us in was very pleasant and he led us back to our bunks. As we passed by the bar and tables, we heard someone yelling at us. We had just walked by the Swedes! We thought we were behind them again and they popped up in the same albergue with us. What were the odds? We said "hello" and told them we would be back out when we got a bed assignment. The host led us back to some bunks and gave us our choice. We chose the last bunkbed on the right side thinking it would be quiet back there. As we got settled in and spread out our normal nightly gear, we started chatting with a guy at the next bunk. He was from Italy but currently lived on an island in Spain. We talked briefly as we both got our bunks situated. He was tending to his poor feet which were having much trouble with blisters. We discussed different options when the sores are on the bottom of the feet, including the suggestion of putting a feminine pad on the bottom of the foot. Hey, whatever works!

We broke our normal routine of taking a shower and changing into evening clothes and decided to just be smelly and enjoy our Swedish friends. We stripped off our sweaty walking clothes and put on evening clothes without a shower in between, our little secret. We were so excited to go back out to visit our favorite Swedes! Each day we expected to have them well ahead of us and not see them again; therefore, every encounter was a blessing to us!

We headed out to visit Lennart and Agneta and asked Lennart what he was sipping on when we sat down. He said it was a lovely Spanish cognac and ordered each of us a cognac as well. How can you turn that down?

We sipped our Spanish cognacs and enjoyed the wonderful friendship we had forged with this beautiful couple! These were the special times on the Camino and we knew it. Lennart told us of many of the different jobs he had done. The one that amazed me the most was that he used to create crossword puzzles. I can't even imagine the intelligence needed to be able to design a crossword puzzle. Lennart and Agneta also told us that they were going to present their Camino at a Pecha Kucha event a couple months after they returned. They explained that it is a presentation of 20 images shown for 20 seconds each. The images advance automatically and you talk along to the images. I thought it was cool that they were going to share their Camino with others when they returned.

The Journey Inward

As we chatted with them, our new Italian friend came out to join us. He was around 5'10", wore earrings in both ears, had a mustache and beard, and his brown hair was shaven except for a Mohawk of inch-long hair across the top of his head. His name was Giacomo. He was from Italy, but currently was a chef on the Spanish island of Mallorca. He chatted with us and, when it was time for dinner, his hospitality background appeared. He brought menus to us and then ordered entrees for the entire table at the bar. It was very unusual but so sweet to order for everyone and take charge of the table with his Spanish. We weren't arguing especially since we all struggled with speaking any Spanish! He finally joined us for dinner and he sat down next to me. I had a fun time getting to know him. He had a sexy voice with an Italian accent and he was definitely alluring.

After a nice dinner, I was tired and decided to head to an early bedtime, while Diane headed back out to socialize at the bar. I curled up in my bed, wrote my journal entry and quickly fell asleep. I woke up in the middle of the night freezing! I was honestly feeling the coldest that I had been on the trip so far. I started to lean over to the end of the bed and grab the normal add-on layers to try to stay warm. I looked at the bunk next to me and saw my new friend, the sexy Italian chef. He was buried in his fluffy, warm sleeping bag fast asleep. Thoughts passed through my mind of crawling in bed with this newly met sexy Italian chef and asking him to keep me warm. As I stood up to get another layer of clothes, I decided to take a chance. I sat on the side of Giacomo's bed and he woke up. I put my index finger to my lips in the universal sign to stay quiet and I leaned over and whispered in his ear to ask him if he could keep me warm. He opened the sleeping bag so I could crawl in. He put his arms around me and his body against me to warm me up. Then I...

...realized that I was just daydreaming and was still shivering in my bed. I cussed my normal self who said my idea was crazy and was too scared to take the chance! Shivering, I pulled every available layer that I could onto me for warmth. The layers were not helping me. I lay there watching him sleep and realized I didn't just want to be warm, but I wanted his strong arms around me. I discovered aloneness in me that I had been unwilling to admit was there. I thought back to my failed attempts at dating the past few years. I desperately yearned for having someone special back home rooting for me daily as I trudged on each hour to reach this crazy goal of walking to Santiago. Someone who would be waiting for me at the airport and squeeze me tight in a big hug, welcoming me back. I realized that, while I was fine living alone, I really wanted to share my life with a special man again. I wiped away my tears and rolled over as I squeezed myself into a little ball to be able to wrap my small fleece blanket around me. The aloneness of my life back home sank in. This was going to be a long night.

Steps: 30,679

The Journey Inward

Rabanal – Molinaseca

Day 21 of 31 (September 20th):
Kilometers: 24.9
Miles: 15.5

We awoke for another day of hiking and chatted with our new friend, the Italian chef, as we all packed up our stuff and prepared to head out. Lennart and Agneta were early risers and we knew they were way ahead of us already. We also knew this was going to be a really tough day of steep ascents and descents, so we decided to send our backpacks ahead and just carry a small bag with us.

We headed out for the day bundled up against the cold weather. It was a long rocky 3.5-mile uphill climb to Foncebadon. Even though it was cold, we worked up a sweat in the climb. My extra layer was cozy in the early morning, but once I got moving and the sun came out, it got very hot and sweaty. Upon entering the town, we found a bar to get a drink and rest a bit. I again traded my leggings for shorts and pulled off my jacket.

Feeling refreshed from our thirst-quenching drink, we continued on. As we walked along, we saw the green valleys and the mountain ahead where the cross at Cruz de Ferro resided. I pondered my thoughts from the previous night. It made me realize that I definitely was tired of being alone, so I knew I needed to let down my guard to be able to open myself up to another relationship.

Diane and I chatted about our relationships again and Diane shared that the guy that she had been attempting to get to ask her out for almost two years had spent close to an hour "sexting" her the previous evening. The timing of his sexual texts was pretty ironic since she was just about to leave a rock at Cruz de Ferro to release the burden of that relationship and move past him. It was just one of those moments when we would look at each other and shrug, wondering why he would even do that now?

We continued to Cruz de Ferro which would be the second highest point in our trip. We were about to follow the Camino tradition of tossing out a stone at the monument to release our life's burdens.

My heart still carried many burdens. After five years, I still had not gotten over my failed marriage and the debt that I carried away from it. I still held bitter feelings of resentment towards Blaine for not helping me pay off this debt. I had such great fears of commitment. After losing my job, I was scared to have the financial commitment of a mortgage. Heck, I was even scared to own a dog with the fear of losing my job and not being able to take care of him/her. Let's not even get started on the fears of commitment to a significant other! Tossing this stone represented getting rid of all of these fears. It was daunting as I climbed up the trail to the cross.

As we approached Cruz de Ferro, I saw the tall wooden pole with a metal cross attached to the top of it. It was surrounded by a mound of stones from years of pilgrims releasing their burdens. Attached to the pole were pieces of clothing and bits of paper. There were different mementos scattered around the pile to represent all the burdens of past pilgrims.

I pulled out my heart-shaped bean stone that I had discovered on the beach. I needed to release all of my failures of the past...all of the failures that weighed me down. It was time to forgive myself for the mistakes that I had made. All of the burdens (the failed marriage, the lost job, the debt, and the aloneness) needed to be released and forgiven so that I could move forward.

Nervously, I approached the cross and pulled out my prayer that I had taken with me. I remembered the prayer that they recited in the movie *The Way* and I found a similar prayer before I left the U.S. and carried it with me. I caressed the stone in my hand as I read my prayer, *"O Lord, may the stone which I bring to this Holy Place be a sign of my pilgrimage to Santiago. When I reach my final judgment, tip the balance of my life in favor of my good deeds. I lay down this token which I carry from Charleston. Please forgive me my sins and help me carry my burden in life. Amen."*

As tears streamed down my cheeks, I tossed my stone onto the large heap of other stones from all the pilgrims that had passed before me and released all of their burdens on the same spot. I closed my eyes and imagined the transfer of these burdens going from inside me over to my sea heart which now sat on the pile of other stones. I felt the weight of my past being released. I breathed in the freedom of releasing these burdens. The feeling was amazing!

I tossed two stones from friends of mine who also asked that their burdens be forgiven and released from their life.

Diane placed her stones on the pile, including a perfectly smooth white and grey sphere which represented letting go of hopes of a relationship with…yep…the "sexter." She said that, after all the sexual texts from him the previous night, he ended it with "lol, just kidding." She explained that it sealed the deal that the little white and grey rock that represented him (he had grey/white hair) had to stay in Spain. She declared that she really needed to let him go; he was playing her like a fiddle but got deeply offended anytime she said so. As long as she was allowing him to keep her as an option, she was never going to move on.

Along with that one, she left a grey stone which represented her ex-husband. She said it was a dark spot left on her heart, thus, the dark grey stone. As she described her stones to me, she said "I need to re-learn my value as a woman, as a partner, and as a person. Allowing these men to have this hold over me has truly been one of the unhealthiest places I had ever been in. My self-perception has been based on these men's affections. It is a pattern I need to figure out how to get rid of." She felt the Camino was definitely speaking to her.

After leaving our burdens behind, we continued on our trail with a lighter step. We started a descent and soon ran across a tiny stop in Manjarin. It was marked by a plethora of colorful flags and distance signs pointing different directions showing that Santiago was 222km away, Roma was 2475 km away and Jerusalem was 5000 km away. Behind the signs was a little shop that sold coffee, snacks, and trinkets, but had no electricity or running water. We wandered through for a quick look and then continued our trek.

After descending for a while, we climbed back up and soon reached the highest point on our journey. After a few very hard and long uphill and downhill climbs we began the difficult descent for the rest of our day's hike. We were able to look down at the next town and saw slate rooftops with a row of flags at the far end. The descent into El Acebo was steep and really brutal as we maneuvered around the washed out gullies. Diane mentioned that they should really try to use some switchbacks to help ease the burden of the steep downhill treks. The steep ascents were difficult on my knees, but the descents were even more brutal, especially since most of the path consisted of gullies where you had to step around the crevasses.

Thankfully, when we approached the village, we got a switchback! They finally realized how helpful a switchback can be! Too bad the previous few miles were not as friendly with more switchbacks and fewer dreadfully steep downhill descents! I was grateful for my trekking poles as I was using them tremendously to help relieve the stress on my knees on the downhill descents.

Once we reached El Acebo, we stopped for a much-needed break. We ambled into a covered outside seating area already crowded with other pilgrims. Finding an empty table, we looked over and saw we had run into our favorite Swedes again! They were just finishing up so we got their recommendations for sandwiches and watched as they left to continue their journey.

The Journey Inward

We put our bags in our seats to save the table and hurried inside to get something to eat. It was highly unusual for us to have anything alcoholic during our walks, but we decided to drink beer to celebrate our difficult descent and, hopefully, it would help us by deadening the pain as we made the steep descents we knew were ahead. We were both very hungry after that hike, so we each opted for a sandwich along with our beer. I had a wonderful sandwich with steak, onions, and cheese. After that difficult climb down, it was so gratifying to sip on a beer and gobble up a steak and onion sandwich on that fantastic Spanish bread! It was indeed the best sandwich on my journey so far!

After a relaxing break, we left El Acebo with a full stomach and a desire to get to our destination for the night. As we walked out of the village along the street, we passed a few grazing sheep next to the road. They appeared unfazed by us as we walked near them. We were walking on the edge of the road, which was dangerous, so we were thankful when our route finally turned off the road and onto a dirt path. It eventually got very steep again as we descended even further down through more rocky paths. We passed through the town of Riego de Ambros and were given words and gestures of encouragement to continue on our Camino.

The path continued to descend steeply through heavy brush with very little shade. I pulled on my light sun shirt to protect me from the hot sun beating down on us. We saw the Swedes up ahead in the distance and eventually caught up with them. We continued our trek ahead of them and soon reached our destination for the night. Entering the outskirts of town, we came to a water fountain. We both filled our bottles and were enthusiastic to have a drink of cold water after our very hot decent. It was unbelievably refreshing! It made the next small trek across the river and into town bearable.

We quickly found our hostel, Hostal El Horno, after crossing the beautiful medieval bridge and were greeted by our gracious host. We had a reservation and our backpacks were shipped ahead to this destination, so he had been expecting us. He swiftly checked us in and showed us to our room, where our backpacks were waiting for us. We didn't have to lug our packs up the two flights of stairs; he had done that for us! What a joy! After all the rugged ascents and descents of the day, it was a blessing not to have that weight on us as we climbed the stairs.

It was a lovely room with bright yellow walls and twin beds with black wrought iron headboards and white bedspreads. The bathroom was white with a bright blue tile floor and blue tile accents on the wall.

We settled into our afternoon routine of showers and washing out our clothes for the day. We had to laugh because we felt such excitement to find real soap and shampoo in our bathroom. It was the little luxuries like these that really made a difference!

We had a small balcony off our room that overlooked the side street. As we were hanging out our clothes to dry, we spotted the Swedes wandering the streets below. We called out a hello to them. I chuckled at seeing them. What are the chances of running into them yet again? The Camino magic was mind-boggling. After walking out on the balcony for just a few minutes, it just so happened that it was the exact same time that our Swedish friends walked by. Amazing!

After getting clean and comfortable, we decided to head out for a drink. We wandered out by the water near the bridge and found a restaurant that overlooked the water. After finding a table, we looked for a waiter to order a drink. We noticed that there seemed to only be one guy taking orders at the outside tables and he seemed to pick the last table seated to wait on. He completely ignored the two of us. After watching this for a while and getting restless, Diane decided to go into the bar and order drinks. She came back out empty-handed and said it appears that the guy serving the tables outside was also the bartender! At this rate, we were not going to get a drink before it was time to start hiking again! We decided to find a more service friendly spot.

While this place had a wonderful river view, what was the point if you couldn't even relax with a drink after a long hot walk? We headed to the next restaurant and, as we turned the corner, guess who we ran into again? It was our favorite Swedes, Lennart and Agneta! Without a delay, Diane and I joined them for a drink and enjoyed the sweet friendship we had with them. Dinner was again delayed until a certain hour, so we had a glass of sangria waiting for the menu to become available.

We had many laughs with our dear friends and thoroughly enjoyed our discussions. It was finally time for dinner and we all decided to stay there for dinner. Diane and I both decided to get the minestrone followed by cod (bacalao), which came in a bowl served directly from the oven and covered by a plate. We were told to leave the plate in place and allow the fish to continue to boil in the bowl for a while. We waited patiently with anticipation. When we were given the direction to finally dig in, we did so with gusto since we were both hungry from the hike. I usually will not order fish since I only like certain kinds, but this was really good!

Lennart had been talking about a yellow shot that he had been served by the waitress earlier, so after dinner, he inquired about another shot of this. We were all served a shot of a yellow liquid which honestly tasted like some kind of household cleaner. I can't say it was good, but Lennart sure liked it. The waitress brought out a bottle labeled with Cardhu Scotch Whiskey which was obviously not what we were drinking. She then told us it was a homemade liqueur called Hierbas and implied that it had marijuana in it. Heck, it smelled like it could have! We enjoyed a second shot to end our evening, making our long trek down the extremely steep inclines worth it! We finished our evening with another goodbye not knowing if we would see our favorite couple again.

Steps: 32,847

Janet Charbonneau

Molinaseca – Cacabelos

Day 22 of 31 (September 21st):
Kilometers: 24.1
Miles: 15.0

We headed out in the morning to more cold weather! As we wandered around the small town, we looked at a couple different options for breakfast. We saw places with outside seating, but it was too darn cold for that! We finally found a place with inside seating just around the corner from our hostel. We went inside to stay warm and order breakfast. We were able to order our normal breakfast of orange juice, coffee, and toast while we enjoyed the warm inside seating for a bit.

With a cold start, we continued along the way and it eventually warmed up for the day. We entered Ponferrada and walked along the roadways inside the town. We passed a gentleman who was interacting with a dog who was behind a fence. He said he walked along the road daily and gave the dog scraps every day. Therefore, he bridged a deep relationship with the dog over time. He continued on with us after visiting the dog and then pulled two sprigs of rosemary off a bush and shared them with us. It smelled so good! We continued to wander through the town with our rosemary attached to our packs. It was such a sweet smell to accompany our walk!

The Journey Inward

As we wandered through the town, we came upon a cool looking castle. We still had a long way to go to our destination for the night, so we decided not to stop to look into it. We were in the "let's hustle and get to our destination so we can relax" mode again.

We continued our trek and at our next stop we ran into the Italian chef, Giacomo; he was leaving the bar as we were getting settled in for a visit. The funny thing was that we could have picked two different places to stop and, even though it was across the street, we picked this one, the same one as Giacomo and his Spanish walking partner, Angel. Angel was over six feet tall with a jolly nature about him. We appeared to be running into them like we were the Swedes! We picked up a drink and continued on our way.

As our trek continued, we got to the next to the last town and ran into a snag! Our route was blocked by a crowd of people gathered for a funeral procession. We saw we couldn't get through the crowd and we looked over to a bar and saw Giacomo and Angel sitting outside at a table. What were the chances? Evidently, they were pretty good on the Camino! We noticed them at the same time that they saw us. Giacomo invited us to join them and, without hesitation, we headed onto the patio and found two seats at their table. We couldn't get anywhere along the streets with this funeral so why not have a beer and chill until the street cleared up?

We enjoyed a beer (Giacomo and Angel's treat) and actually chilled for some time on our journey with no sense of hurry. This was two days in a row that we actually stopped midday and had a beer. It was very different from what we usually did. We rarely had a beer midday.

Giacomo told us that he and Angel had met on their first day on the Camino after starting in Leon. They hit it off and had been walking together ever since. After chatting with them for a while, we all headed out for our destination. We were headed to the same town as our planned stop for the day. I walked along with Giacomo and we chatted, but eventually, Diane and I went ahead of them. When we got to Cacabelos, we looked for a hotel we had seen advertised along the way and found out they were full. We continued to look around and found an albergue that had a private room.

As we waited to be checked in, I looked at Diane with horror. One of her eyes was bright red with blood! Startled, she asked me what was wrong. I told her and she explained that she gets hematomas often in her eyes. It still freaked me out. After losing my brother to an aneurysm, something that looked like it had ruptured in her head was disconcerting. She told me that it would be OK and to not worry about it. Easy for her to say!

Later that day, we found Giacomo doing laundry, so he was staying in the same building; he was in the albergue instead of the hostel. It was funny that we ended up in the same place again.

After getting settled into our room, we sat outside at a table in the courtyard drinking sangrias. Giacomo came up, after having walked around the town, and recommended a nice restaurant. So we splurged and headed to the restaurant around the corner. Giacomo walked with us and translated the menu for both of us before Diane and I went inside. We both ordered the steak and decided we wanted the notorious French fries for a second item. The steak came out with a buttery cheese sauce on it. Our fries were homemade and we had some hearty bread and wine along with it. Wow, was that steak good! It was delightful to deviate from our normal pilgrim's meal; it didn't hurt that the waiter once again was a good looking Spaniard!

Steps: 32,666

Cacabelos – Ambasmestas

Day 23 of 31 (September 22nd):
Kilometers: 24.7
Miles: 15.3

We both woke up and were moving slowly for the morning. We were 23 days into the hike and it was starting to take a toll on us. We desperately needed to take a rest day but we were ready to finish the hike, so we kept hiking onward each day to get there sooner. We were two stubborn, determined women who were ready to reach our destination, but we still had 9 days to go.

Our day started with our usual toast, juice, and coffee for breakfast at our hostel to prepare us for the walk. We headed out thankful that it wasn't as cold as the previous mornings. Our trek to Villafranca was all uphill but the scenery with vineyards was welcoming after all the days of the nothingness of the Meseta. We passed another church and castle heading into town. The town was quaint looking, but as we wandered through it, we lost our arrows. We ran into another couple who were also looking for the arrows, so the four of us backtracked a short ways and then realized we had missed the arrow showing us to take a right and go down some stairs. As we were searching for our route, we compared our intended routes; that couple planned to walk along the highway and we were planning on taking a different route.

Before heading out of town, we stopped for a drink and a rest which ended up being a smart idea. We crossed the bridge heading out of town and came to a point where there were different path options. This is where I should have stopped Diane and compared books! I had seen these options a few days prior and during a couple of previous days when Diane said we were taking a scenic option, I had asked her if it was the one that was a lot steeper than the other one. I had this steep optional route on my brain. She would always say, "no, it is not that one." Well, today was the day. What I didn't realize was that my guidebook showed only two options, while her guidebook showed three options! The descriptions of each differed between our books.

As we got to the decision point, my book showed the easier route along the highway to the left and described it this way:

"Much of the day's walking will be on a track parallel to the highway, with crash barriers providing protection from traffic. Because of the superhighway flyover passing above, the traffic on the old highway is fairly light."

While Diane's book described it as having dangerous bends, told you to stay alert with the traffic and talked about it being a greater risk of injury.

For option 2, my book said it was a "pass through the mountains, high difficulty". Diane's book said this was the intermediate option and describes it this way:

"This scenic route is very beautiful and makes the most of the early morning sun which doesn't penetrate into the lower Valcarce valley until later in the day. The steep climb up (400m) is rewarded with wonderful views back over Villafranca but you will need to allow an extra hour or two for this longer route with the extra ascent and steep descent it involves. Its use is, inexplicably, discouraged by locals."

It also explained that "if the warning signs for fitness worry you, remember that if you made it this far you should encounter no undue problems."

Her guidebook labeled the third option as "for experienced walkers only." Therefore, when I said not to go on the difficult option, she came back and told me that it was not the difficult option (according to her book.) She read the easy option as being very dangerous and evidently ignored the parts of her book that said this intermediate option would take an extra hour or two and that you needed to take snacks and water along the way with you. Not knowing our guidebooks were so different, she took us on what she thought was the safest route, which ended up being the high difficulty route described by my book and the one I had been hoping to avoid for days.

The first quarter mile was straight up and Diane, who was like a mountain goat, just shimmied up it quickly. I found it much more difficult and again questioned that she was taking us on the difficult route. She got frustrated and said the difficult route was to the left at our decision point and that this first little section was the toughest part since that is what her guidebook said. What she didn't realize was that her chosen route was uphill the entire way until we got to the end where we encountered a very steep descent!

I reached the top of the first quarter mile, stopped, and took a deep breath. I was already starting to question this route. While the next section wasn't straight up like the first quarter, it still was an ascending climb. Diane continued to trek ahead and I continued on but fell back considerably from her. This route was 7.2 miles to Trabadelo and the first 5 miles of it were uphill. We continued walking up and got a very nice view of Villafranca in the valley. The view was striking but it really wasn't striking enough to warrant this hike uphill! I stopped again to enjoy the view and seriously considered turning around. I knew we still had a very long way to go and it continued to be uphill. I also knew that there was an easier route below that would be fairly flat. I was very frustrated that I had not questioned this route further with Diane and had just trusted her judgement. I had no idea why she thought this was an easy route! I stood there debating what to do. I had woken up with very little energy and was in no mood for this ridiculous route which could have been avoided. I was getting angry that I had just continued to follow Diane's route without questioning it.

Diane was much further ahead of me and I didn't want to split us up. Against my better judgement, I continued on. Up, up, up we went and just when we thought we would start descending, we would go up again! I believe Diane got to the point where she realized the route was more difficult than she expected. I was miserable as we continued to climb, knowing there was an easier route. We got lost a couple of times and had to stop to figure out the route. The second time, we ran across a guy who was trying to figure out the route as well, but he is the ONLY person we encountered on this route!

We finally got to our descending point down the mountain. Down, down, down we went. While ascents were difficult, the steep descents were excruciating on my knees! I had to walk slowly and concentrate on being careful where I stepped to ensure a solid footing. Just as I cussed Diane going up the mountain, I cussed her even more as I descended the steep mountain!

Much of the steep descent was on a paved road and then, when we got to the end, it was a dirt path with a harshly steep descent into Trabadelo. Once we got into town, we looked for a place to grab a bite to eat. We realized that this route dropped us off at the far end of town and we had missed all of the bars. We were too exhausted to backtrack. We found an albergue with a drink machine and got an Aquarius. I chugged mine down as we rested outside of the albergue and I went back in to get a second one. I was extremely hot, thirsty, and exhausted!

As we sat there resting, the couple that we had encountered in Villafranca passed us. Again, I thought, what are the chances of running across them during the ten minutes we sat resting? I believe it was the Camino talking to us again. You could tell that they had just stopped and were well rested. Diane and I decided they had most likely come from a rest stop in the same town where they had time to eat a nice meal, all in the same amount of time that it took us to walk our "intermediate" route.

Boy, was I angry that we could have been to our albergue for the night already! We still had another 3 miles to walk! I was completely exhausted and was not even sure how my legs were still moving; they felt like Jell-O. I trudged along slowly and painfully but was rewarded by having a river running along the left side of the road for most of the route. I concentrated on the sound of the water rustling over rocks, which soothed me as we trekked our last three miles for the day. I always find water very comforting, so I was grateful for the peaceful water which carried me to our albergue.

They say that the Camino will provide and it did, indeed, provide me with a mental river retreat to assist me in finishing the day's hike.

As we approached Ambasmestas, I was hoping that our hostel would sit looking over the river, but we found our hostel on the right side of the road away from the river. We entered CTR Ambasmestas via the bar. I considered stopping right there, but we went to find the front desk. We asked at the bar where we could check in. They brought us up some stairs and asked if we had a reservation. We did, so they got our keys for us and took us to our room, telling us to just pay in the morning. Wow, pay in the morning? Who does that nowadays?

It was a nice room and we were happy to have a private room after our long, hot hike for the day. The bathroom had a slanted ceiling with rich, dark wood and a skylight set into it which opened and allowed us to breathe the fresh air. We took our showers, washed our clothes and went back down to the bar. We ordered our wine and it was one Euro per glass, just over $1 US! That was my kind of prices, plus it was a very good glass of wine! I was hungry and it would be a while before they would be serving dinner, so I grabbed some chips to munch on. I was glad I did all that walking to be able to snack before dinner! It was always the most tremendous feeling to have accomplished the hike for the day and finally relax.

As we sipped on our red wine, we discussed the route we had taken that day. Diane knew I had been extremely frustrated with the route, but I was not one to argue. We both described what our guidebooks had stated and we realized that the two books did not match in the number of routes available along with the descriptions of each. Diane finally understood my questioning her route decision and why I had been so frustrated. We agreed that in the future if we did not agree on our routes, then we would take a few minutes to compare guidebooks.

We decided to stay at the hostel for the pilgrim's meal. I had a very different first course: peas and ham. For those that know me, you know that I hate peas. The difference was that these were fresh, crisp peas, unlike canned peas, and this dish was awesome! Of course, it was accompanied by the usual bread and wine. This section of Spain had much heartier, coarser bread. It was interesting to watch the bread and meals change as we traveled through the different regions! My second course was pork and chunks of potatoes. The dessert was one of the best on the trail; it was a dark chocolate mousse in a wafer cup. Now I am not big on sweets, but I have to say that this dark chocolate with the red wine made the hike that day well worth it! And that definitely spoke volumes after that difficult hike! As exhausted as I was after our hike, I felt that this chocolate and red wine combination was better than sex at this point.

Steps: 28,290

The Journey Inward

Ambasmestas – O Cebreiro

Day 24 of 31 (September 23rd):
Kilometers: 13.3
Miles: 8.3

It was going to be a short day, but we knew that we would have a very difficult final ascent to O Cebreiro, so we purposely made it a short day distance-wise. We had breakfast at the hostel and then checked out of our room and paid our bill for our overnight stay.

The first part of our hike was a very lovely one. We walked along the road, but the river was along the left side of the road for most of it. It was a very peaceful walk with the soothing water next to us. The scenery was becoming delightful again with rolling hills, trees, and cows along the way. We were starting to enter the Galacia section of the Camino which would provide more forests, rivers, and possibly more rain. The scenery was a welcomed sight after the many days on the flat, barren Meseta.

The first town we went through was Vega de Valcarce. It would be the last town with a bank for a while, so we stopped to withdraw money. It took us a couple of tries to access an ATM since the first one was out of order. Thankfully, we were successful with the next one down the street. It was always a bit nerve-racking when the ATM you try to use does not work and you don't know if there is another one in town! We also found a small market to buy drinks and snacks.

The walk was a very pleasant one as we passed cows in the meadows as well as right next to the road. The stream continued to weave in and out, sometimes next to the road and sometimes down in the valley. I was excited every time the stream came next to the road, especially when it is was bubbling over some rocks. This was the third section of the Camino that was known to be for the soul. The soothing babbling brook sounds were indeed good for my soul!

We walked past a few horses along this route. It was a delightful walk…until it was time to go straight up the rocky dirt path! We knew it was coming. We knew we would have a very steep ascent up to O Cebreiro and it was indeed! O Cebreiro was our destination for the day since we knew it was going to be so steep to get there. We slowly climbed the couple of miles to La Faba and then stopped in the small town for an Aquarius. After a short break, we continued the trek for the next three miles going straight up the mountain. The thought that kept me going was that it was a short day and the uphill climb would end soon. Up, up, up we went! We passed the marker decorated in red, blue, and yellow symbols that officially stated that we had passed into the Galicia region. It was a grueling ascent, but we slowly plodded on.

We entered O Cebriero around 1:00 p.m. which was one of our earliest days so far. As we walked into town we noticed tour buses parked along the way. I was wondering if they were just in town for a short visit or overnight. We continued through town and found a hostel, Casa Carolo, for the night. We were happy to find a place to stay in a private room that was available so early in the day.

One of the nice perks was that there was a little store next to it that would wash and dry laundry for 8 Euros and it would be done in an hour! Jackpot! We took our showers, gathered our laundry, and dropped it off to be washed.

It was then on to find a drink and possibly some food. Thankfully, the crowds were not bad and it looked like the buses were starting to leave. We wandered through a couple of tourist shops and I bought a little keychain with the Camino symbol on the front and O Cebreiro written on the back. Next, we searched for a good place to relax. We found a restaurant that served food all day and we were able to get a pilgrim's menu at 3:00 in the afternoon! Jackpot again! We had to wait for a table, but it wasn't too long before we were finally sitting and enjoying our meal.

When we were finished eating, we decided to visit the other shops in town. Being in Galicia province, the Celtic influence was very apparent in this hamlet. Celtic music was playing in the shops and many of the souvenirs had Celtic symbols on them. It was starting to cool down and was becoming quite chilly. We walked across the street and into a quaint little shop with many interesting things to browse. What caught my immediate attention was a nice fleece jacket! It looked warm and I was pretty tired of being cold on this trip. The fleece jacket was navy blue with a yellow Camino symbol on it and the words "Camino de Santiago" embroidered underneath. I tried it on and was finally warm! SOLD! This was exactly what I had been looking for the past week. I was ecstatic to finally be warm! It wasn't too heavy and I had used stuff in the backpack, so I thought it would fit in it. At this point, I didn't care...I just really wanted to be warm! I continued to browse through the shop as Diane picked out a souvenir for one of her daughters.

After we both made our purchases, we wandered around the rest of the small town. We found a couple of places to possibly have breakfast as well as the municipal albergue with its weird alien person symbol on the sign. We headed back to pick up our laundry. It was ready when we got there. We returned to our hostel and looked out over the valley. Across the street from the hostel, there were beautiful fir trees that reminded me of Christmas trees back home. We were at the top of the mountain and the views below were phenomenal! The scenery was of rolling hills and valleys consisting of green forests, farmland, and pastures. After so much nothingness in the Meseta, these views were so special to us! They soothed the soul!

We walked back to the room to relax and take a nap. After a couple of hours, we finally dragged ourselves out of bed and decided to go out for a drink. We went out to one of the places we had seen earlier and ordered a glass of wine. We didn't feel like socializing, so we decided that it was time to head back to the hostel and go to bed. We were in bed by 9:00 p.m. with no internet available in our room. It was one of our earliest nights. Without internet, we decided to hit the sack and catch up on some sleep!

Steps: 17,979

O Cebreiro – Triacastela

Day 25 of 31 (September 24th):
Kilometers: 20.7
Miles: 12.9

After getting dressed and packing our backpacks, we headed out for some breakfast. In the entire town, only one little bar was open. It was the same one where we had drinks the previous evening. We walked into a full house! We stood by the bar trying to get service which was difficult as there was only one woman waiting on a non-stop barrage of pilgrims looking for coffee. After waiting for a while, we split up. I scouted out a table while Diane ordered our breakfast. I managed to find a table as another group was leaving. We ended up sharing that table with another couple of people who were looking for a spot as well.

    As we finally got a chance to eat our breakfast, we saw Giacomo again! He came over to our table and we chatted about our destination. We were headed to the same town but we were staying at different places again, so we decided we would try to catch up there if we could. We hurriedly ate our breakfast and then quickly exited to get out of the crowd.

    We went up the path near the municipal albergue but the arrows showed us to go up the mountain. We started up and then crossed over the road to see the view. We had gotten an early start so were fortunate enough to see the amazing sunrise; it was full of oranges and yellows. As we went back to our route, we saw that the other side of the road overlooked the mountains and valleys that were filled with low-hanging clouds. It was an eerie sight to see the ocean of clouds surrounding the mountains poking through.

After enjoying the extraordinary sunrise, we continued to follow the yellow arrows. Our guidebooks said to either follow along near the municipal albergue or to head up on the dirt path left of there and climb the mountain. We followed the arrows up the mountain and got half way up and ran out of arrows. We had no clue if we were on the correct route. Plus the path had been dug up by bulldozers. We finally stopped a guy on his bulldozer and asked if we were still on the Camino. He said we were and pointed us in the right direction along the freshly bulldozed road. We continued on and then a young guy and his mother caught up with us. We were very unsure if we were on the correct path because we were not seeing the Camino arrows. They asked us if we were going in the right direction and we were very honest and told them we had no idea if we were right!

The young guy's mother had told him they should have taken the right arrow near the municipal albergue and we had wondered the same thing. We all plodded on...eventually, after many doubts, our dirt path ran into another dirt path and a couple of pilgrims were also along that path! We felt that we were no longer lost! Saved!

We continued on the trail and our path was constantly uphill. We had really expected more downhill today since the final destination was after another steep descent so the constant ascents were not what we were expecting at all! What the heck! For a bit, we paralleled a road and then the path went straight uphill as the road beside it curved gently ahead. We saw an older lady who was in her 70s or 80s pulling a rolling suitcase behind her. She attempted the rocky uphill climb and then turned around and ran into us. She asked if the parallel road would take her to the same area as the path. It was a request in Spanish and we could only guess at the question. Also, having no idea what lay ahead, we had no clue how to answer it. So she decided to walk along the road and we forged ahead on the "straight up the rocky path" route. We walked up the steep trail and then back down another steep descent and eventually met up with the road again. We crossed the road to see a statue of a pilgrim who appeared to be trudging on against the wind.

As we finished our rest near the statue, we looked at the road and the little old lady who took the route along the road was trudging by with her rolling suitcase. Why had I just struggled up the very steep ascent and then again the steep descent when we could have just walked along the nice steady road instead? Maybe the route we took was safer than walking along the road. I was going to go with that explanation to justify having walked over the large hill for no reason.

We trekked on along the road and then followed a parallel trail alongside it. The trail eventually went up an extremely steep rocky hill. Diane shimmied up it like her usual mountain goat self and I trudged very slowly to the top…slow and steady. When I got to the top I noticed a nice bar awaited to reward you for that climb. I went in for a cold drink and ran into one of the couples that we had dinner with in Reliegos. I chatted with them as I waited in line. When I had received my drink, I went out to find Diane.

We sat at one of the tables and chatted for a bit. After a short rest, we were ready to go. As we were starting to head out, we watched another elderly lady in her 70s or 80s trudge up that rocky steep hill as she pulled her rolling suitcase behind her. What was it with elderly ladies and rolling suitcases along this stretch? Once she reached the top, you could see that she was shocked that there was a nice café at the top of the climb. You could see the shock and sense of accomplishment in the same face. It was cool to see her determination pay off! I definitely knew the feeling!

The scenery was quite a welcome change as we walked through rolling hills of green pastures dotted with cows. We passed through quaint little towns where everyone seemed to have barns filled with cows. Cows seemed to be the theme of the day. We had a few steep descents, which were very difficult on my knees, so I was thankful every time the descent was gradual!

The Camino was getting crowded now that we were getting close to the 100 km mark. To get your Compostela in Santiago you had to walk the last 100 km, so many people will start walking near that 100 km mark. While walking past one of the bars today, we saw a crowd of people walk out. You could tell the newbies to the Camino. They were full of energy and chatty. They were wearing nice clean clothes and you could see their backpacks lacked use or they just carried a minimal day pack. Many of the women wore makeup. With one glance you could tell that this group was of the newbie class.

As we walked by them, I overheard one of the women complain in a very loud voice that she wanted to bring another one of whatever she ate because it was so good but that her male friend would not allow her to bring a beer along with it on the hike. She seemed to just be here for a party and not a serious hike. She was very annoying. Diane and I looked at each other and we both managed to walk by without slapping her. Obviously, she had no respect for this journey...just a party time for her. After walking for so many days on this journey, her disrespect was appalling. It was eye-opening to see the difference in people who were appearing on the Camino as we approached Santiago. We scurried past them quickly to get them out of our range and not have to deal with them again!

We finally arrived in Triacastela and went looking for a place to stay. We found Berce do Caminho and were able to get two beds for the night. We had a room with only five beds (two bunk beds and a single), so at least it wasn't too bad as far as sharing with others. There were two bathrooms available so we both got our stuff together to take a shower and get ready for the evening.

After our shower and finding a place to wash and hang our clothes, we headed out looking for a place to relax. We were in luck! The restaurant we went to had dinner available and it was only 3:00 p.m.! We were so excited to be able to eat so early. We wished more areas in Spain would have dinner at earlier times like this place did. We sat outside in the sunshine and had an outstanding meal. Diane shared her salmon with a street cat who wouldn't budge from under our

The Journey Inward

table. Obviously, it was a smart cat; Diane was eating salmon! As we were finishing up our pilgrim's meal, Giacomo walked by us. It was a small world. The Camino magic connected us again! He joined us and we chatted for a bit. Eventually, Angel came up to join him and they ended up going to another table to have dinner.

While they were eating their early dinner, we walked around the town and found a Pharmacia where Diane could get the things she needed. After our shopping was complete, we headed back out to the restaurant and saw that Giacomo and Angel were still eating. We joined them at their table and ordered a glass of sangria for each of us. Those two were so much fun to be around! Diane sat next to Angel and they seemed able to be able to communicate some since Angel only knew Spanish and Diane had a little experience with Spanish. I sat next to Giacomo thankful that he could speak English since I did not understand Spanish at all. We spent a little time attempting to connect via the WhatsApp app. We finally got it working and were excited to be able to keep up with each other for the rest of the trip.

Giacomo had found a wild porcini mushroom along his hike that day and he was going to add it to a homemade dinner that evening. We accepted his invitation to a late dinner together. We headed back to the albergue to retrieve our dried laundry and to relax for a bit. When we got close to our timeframe for our late dinner, we headed out to find the albergue where our friends were staying. They met us at the door and led us to the kitchen. Giacomo was busy cooking using this fresh mushroom along with broth, pasta, tomatoes, bacon, and garlic. When he finished, he served the four of us a late dinner. It ended up being Giacomo, me, Diane, and his friend Lara from Italy who was also a chef. Angel was not confident enough to join us. In fact, he said he didn't want to die from a mysterious mushroom so he was not going to eat it. Haha! No loyalty! Evidently, we trusted Giacomo much more than his new Spanish friend did. The pasta was delicious and we had a great time at dinner.

Steps: 30,276

Janet Charbonneau

Triacastela – Sarria

Day 26 of 31(September 25th):
Kilometers: 18.7
Miles: 11.6

For breakfast, we headed back to the same restaurant where we ate dinner. They had a table inside and we got our usual breakfast of toast and coffee or juice. After we were finished with breakfast, we paid at the bar and headed out for the day.

The ascents were very hard for me on this day. I was just extremely tired. It was one of those days where the continuous walking was taking a toll on me. Thankfully, we had a short hiking day. Our day was full of clouds and cows! We had the amazing sight of being above the clouds and could see them hovering over the valleys below. It was quite a unique view to be above the clouds. As we descended, we ended up in the clouds, having to walk through the fog. It was a very wet walk and we were looking forward to finally getting either above the clouds again or underneath them. We continued our descent and ended up under the clouds with no more fog and the ability to see where we were going!

We ran into all kinds of cows today. We saw brown ones with really long curvy horns, white ones with black hooves covered in mud, and black and white spotted ones. They were all close to our path. At one point a single gentleman was herding some black and white cows and we had to stop to wait for them to mosey along. We couldn't pass them on the narrow pathway, so we plodded on slowly behind them for a while. They eventually came to their destination and sauntered off to the right side of the road as we finally hiked on ahead at a regular pace.

Our route took us into very few towns for the day. The towns that were available were often from a detour to the walking path. As we were walking, we ran into a lady from West Palm Beach, Florida. Her name was Suzanne. She was walking with a friend of hers but their walking styles were very different. She walked slower than her friend but at a steady pace with fewer stops. Her friend had a very fast pace but would stop for very long coffee breaks. So they came to an agreement that they would walk separately and just end up meeting up and staying in the same place for the night.

As we were walking along with her and hearing her story, she ran across a couple that she had met on her first day out. She had started in Leon by herself with plans to meet up with her friend a couple of days later. She had started on her hike alone but wanted to find someone else walking the Camino in order to have a walking partner on the first day and feel like she was on the right track. Therefore, she began searching for anyone with a backpack! She ran across this couple who only spoke Spanish. Suzanne did not know Spanish so they did the best they could with sign language. She hadn't seen this couple since that first day where they had helped each other get through the day and here she was nine days later and ran into the same couple! It is so cool how we continue to run into the same people out here. Truly amazing! She stopped to talk to her friends and Diane and I continued on.

We kept on walking and eventually the young German couple, who passed us yesterday, passed us again. You could hear the "click, click click" of their walking sticks in unison as they approached and we knew who it was without even looking. We wondered what it was with the Germans and their fast-paced marching. They passed us and went on clicking in unison. Diane said "I bet sex is boring" and I knew she was talking about this couple and laughed.

We got to Sarria before 1:00 p.m. and found our hostel, Pension A Pedra, for the night. The owner was at the bar and checked us in when we arrived. He spoke English very well and was extremely welcoming to us! We had shipped our bags ahead and he told us that our bags had not yet arrived. He told us the timing was typical and we should expect them within the next couple of hours. We ordered a Tinto de Verano while we waited for our backpacks.

As we were standing at the bar, the girl from Poland appeared. She asked about a room and was told the rates of the albergue. When she was told the rate for the night, she declined because it was 5 Euros above her budget. She had a 15 Euro budget and this would have gone over her budget. She was doing so well at that but I wanted her to have a nice place to stay for the night, so I offered to pay for the 5 Euro difference so she could stay in the albergue for the night. She declined. She wanted to stay in her budget and not get help. I was really disappointed but I had to honor her wishes.

When our drinks came, the owner told us to go through the albergue next door (which he also ran) and to take our drinks outside to the lounge chairs and to relax. How could we refuse that! Wow, it was a pleasure! We were able to take our drinks out of the bar, go through the adjoining albergue, and wander through the backyard with lush green grass and lounge chairs! It was a beautiful lush garden which we had not seen much of here. We sat on the lounge chairs and actually relaxed for a bit. It was heaven!

We noticed a locked storage space in the back of the albergue. We assumed it was for cyclists to lock up their bikes but the manager of the albergue said that it was for "bad pilgrims." We all laughed.

After a while, the owner came out and told us that our backpacks had arrived. We went back to the bar and the lady at the bar showed us where our bags were and then told the owner to carry them up for us. We had to go up three flights of stairs and she told him to take both of our backpacks up to our room! Wow, we were so thankful!

The Journey Inward

While it was a small act of kindness for him, it was huge for us to not have to lug our backpacks up three flights of stairs. We were seeing that it was the small things that we were grateful for during this journey.

We followed our normal routine and took our showers. It was still very quiet on that floor since the other rooms had not been occupied yet. There was a washer and dryer in the adjoining albergue so we took advantage of it and washed and dried some of our laundry. It was a nice addition to our stay!

After getting our clothes washed and dried, we wandered into town. We were looking for a good place to eat. One of the guys we had run into told us about a place that served octopus but I really wasn't into that, so we continued to follow the path into town. We came to a place that had many restaurants overlooking the beautiful river that ran through the town. As we wandered through each restaurant, we looked at the menu. We found an Italian restaurant that was busy and looked like it had good pizzas. We sat down and ordered sangrias to get us started. You can't go wrong with a sangria start!

I ordered a pizza with prosciutto ham, chorizo, mozzarella cheese, and onion on it. Diane ordered a Caprese salad along with a pizza. Giacomo contacted me via WhatsApp and wanted to see where we were. I told him our location as best as I could with the direction we walked. We sat waiting for our food. Diane got the Caprese salad first and was wondering how she was going to eat her pizza since this already looked like dinner. We eventually got our pizzas and they looked awesome. I love a thin crust pizza and it was the perfect thin crust with the edges lightly brown so you knew it was going to be a nice crunchy crust. It was phenomenal! First of all, it was so refreshing to have something different besides a pilgrim's meal and, second, it was an incredible pizza! YUM!! As we were starting to eat our pizzas, Giacomo showed up. It was cool that he managed to find us!

We immediately offered slices of pizza from both of our pizzas. He selected a piece of pizza from Diane's pizza first. After finishing that and seeing I had a long way to go with mine, he then took a slice of my pizza. The owner came back out and chatted with us and Giacomo. Since Giacomo grew up in Italy and was also a chef, he immediately connected with the owner and they chatted for a while...in Italian! The owner was actually from Switzerland and had married an Italian woman and then moved to Spain to open a pizzeria! After their chat, the owner disappeared inside and then came back out with shots of Limoncello for each of us! Sweet! We, of course, had to guzzle those shots before we left this awesome pizza joint.

Neither of us could finish our pizzas so we asked for a leftovers box and decided we would have leftover pizza for breakfast. You can't go wrong with leftover pizza for breakfast and, if you get a pizza this good after all those pilgrim's meals, then you definitely are not going to waste it! Giacomo had ordered the limoncello since we had told him the story of the Italian biker calling Diane "limoncello." Giacomo pointed to Diane's hair and said that the man was calling her the equivalent to "blondie"....now we knew!

It was Angel's birthday so we wanted to wish him a Happy Birthday. Giacomo led us to the albergue that they were staying in. As we followed Giacomo, we went up some stairs and then up more stairs. All I could think of is that we had to climb all of those stairs again in the morning since the Camino continued on this route! Ugh! When we reached their albergue, Giacomo found Angel and we left to get a drink to celebrate his birthday.

Along the way, they wanted to stop at a tourist shop. Angel wanted to start sending his pack ahead and he wanted to buy a smaller daypack to carry. Giacomo browsed and bought a couple of magnets as he was in there and then we left for a drink. We wandered the streets and ended up in the same strip where we had eaten dinner. I was wondering if we were going to end up at the same place, but they finally found a place to have a drink before coming across the pizza place again. While we were enjoying our drinks, Giacomo opened the package from the store and gave both Diane and me a

The Journey Inward

Camino magnet. He had purchased those magnets for us! That was so sweet of him!

After our drinks, we decided we all needed to go back and try to get some sleep. Diane and I had to remember how in the world we had gotten to this section of town, but we managed to negotiate the streets looking for familiar places and get back to our albergue.

Steps: 30,279

Janet Charbonneau

Sarria – Portomarin

Day 27 of 31 (September 26th):
Kilometers: 22
Miles: 13.7

We started our day by eating the awesome leftover pizza from dinner the night before. It has to be a great day when you can start it with leftover pizza! We attempted to find a Jacotrans form to send our packs ahead again but couldn't find any at the hostel or adjoining albergue. We settled on carrying our packs for the day. On the way through town, we stopped for our normal coffee and juice, minus the toast since we had already eaten pizza.

After our drinks, we climbed all those stairs again that we had climbed the night before, which was harder since we were carrying our packs. We finally got to the top of the stairs and headed out of town. We had a very chatty crew walking next to us heading out of town. You could immediately tell a difference. The trek was getting very full of people who you could tell were the "last 100 kilometers" newbies; they were wearing daypacks, clean sneakers, and dress shoes, were very chatty, and acted like they had no idea why they were walking the trail. It was such a different experience! These people were on a mission to just walk and finish the trail to get a piece of paper to say you walked this trail. I totally disagree with this requirement. 100 kilometers? This was equivalent to just over 62 miles. Is that really enough to qualify for a certificate of any accomplishment? And then to make it worse, you get all these tour buses who drop off their groups for a morning jaunt. They meet at a point where they receive lunch and the buses take you further on to another drop off point. These people do not meet the requirements at all, but they get their two stamps a day! Is this really qualifying them for the Compostella? This was the most frustrating part of our trip. The massive groups of people trekking along to get the piece of paper at the end. I believed the requirements were far too lenient!

It was incredibly annoying on the hike that day with so many new people who talked way too much! They were wearing their new clothing, sending their backpacks or luggage ahead, and never experienced the heavy burden of carrying their backpacks while hiking up a steep mountain. They wore makeup and were all posh, yet barely made their requirements to get their Compostela. It was so frustrating to walk with these people! It was such a difference on the trail and so irritating! Diane admitted wanting to stick her trekking pole in front of their path to trip them. Of course, she felt bad for judging their "Way."

As we neared the 100K mark, a busload of people was let out in front of us and they marched through that historic waypoint, totally oblivious of what it represented. To those of us who had walked for over 25 days, it was a tremendous accomplishment! We were four days from finally accomplishing our goals! For Diane and me, it was extremely exciting! Only four days left! It was very aggravating to see all these clueless people while we had the end in sight and were wildly anticipating accomplishing our goal!

We ran into Giacomo at one of the rest stops. I was hoping to use the restroom there, but it consisted of a portable toilet. I didn't need to pee that bad! We saw the crowds descend and decided to not even stop for a drink. We told Giacomo we would see him down the road and we headed out again. We quickly walked past the new chatty crowd on the trail. Damn, they were annoying! They also had no clue about etiquette and would just stop to chat in the middle of the walkway. You would practically run into them as they stopped to chat. We walked as fast as we could to get past all of them and have the trail to ourselves again!

We walked through two more towns and kept on walking as fast as we could. There were children running amok like they were at an amusement park. It was extremely distracting! Oh God, please get these people off the trail!

We came across a young man dressed in traditional Gaelic clothing playing bagpipes in the middle of a stretch of forest, an eerie tune as we wandered along the path in the forest. He was in the middle of nowhere! It was thrilling to hear his bagpipes as we approached him and unique for him to be playing in a random section of the Camino to encourage our trek. About ten minutes later, we reached the 100-kilometer marker. We were ecstatic to have made it that far! As we entered the next town, we ran across an ostrich behind a chain link fence; we never knew what you would run across out there.

We trekked on, took a quick bathroom break in the next town and then kept on going. There was no rest for the weary! We ran across a stopped bus handing out lunches to their people walking the trail. Again, we were annoyed with these tour bus pilgrims. We finally realized the last 100K was going to be really difficult! It was so peaceful up until this time.

Diane really nailed it when she said this was the spiritual part; we had to dig deep and ignore all the obnoxious people on the trail. We had to dig deep and not judge these people but acknowledge their desire to accomplish this task. That in itself was extremely difficult! They were so offensive that to accept them was very daunting!

As we approached Portomarin, we came upon a bridge and on our side of the bridge was a roadblock from a family reunion, at least that is what it appeared to be! Literally, they all gathered and chatted and blocked the way to town. We were truly at our wit's end at this point! Ugh! We finally had to be vocal with "Excuse Me" as we squeezed through them. We were ready to get into the town and relax! We hoped that there was a place to stay and that they had not booked the entire town ahead of time!

We finally made it to town and then had what looked like 100 steps to get up into the town. It was actually more like 50 steps and a hefty ascent but we finally made it. We got to our hostel, Ultreia, and found that we did indeed have a private double room but had a shared bathroom which was EXTREMELY small! The two beds were actually a bunk bed and the room was fairly small but we were thankful to have a room where it was just the two of us! We had a nice shared porch where we could sit in the afternoon sun. We went to take a shower and this was the most uncomfortable that I had been the whole trip. There was nowhere to get dressed when you got out of the shower and it was a shared bathroom for both men and women. I wandered out of the shower in my towel and went into a toilet stall to get dressed. Thankfully I did not run into any men along the way, but when I got to that stall, I really didn't have much more room! Good grief! I was considering wandering back to my room in a towel but did not want to run into the new group of people who had just arrived!

We hand-washed our clothes and found a rack outside to dry them. We were on the second floor and, thankfully, the rack was on that floor and not overhanging to the first floor. There would be no issues dropping our clothes onto the first floor! While we were doing our normal Camino routines, I got a message from Giacomo. He asked if we were in Portomarin for the night. When I told him that we were in Portomarin, he invited us to dinner. He was cooking for the group of pilgrims who I had nicknamed "Giacomo's and Angel's entourage". They always coordinated which albergue that they would stay at together each night.

We were hungry, so we went to find a place to eat since it was mid-afternoon and Giacomo was not cooking until later in the evening. We ended up in the market and decided to just buy meat and cheese, and head back to the hostel. We wandered through the market and bought meat, cheese, and bread. I found a lovely 2008 Rioja for around $8 and it was a really good quality wine! The others were around $2. I wished the wine was that inexpensive in the US!

As we went to check out, we saw Giacomo enter the store. I stayed in line to check out while Diane went to give Giacomo a hard time since his dinner time was coming up. He had invited us to dinner and he was running late. He changed the dinner time from 8:00 p.m. to 9:00 p.m. and we said we would see him soon.

We headed back to the hostel and went to see what amenities we could find in the kitchen. We did not find a whole lot, just plates and a knife to cut the meat. We got some glasses for the wine and found a wine opener. The kitchen amenities were very sparse! We managed to have a lovely first dinner with a sandwich of crusty bread, meat, cheese, and mustard; Diane had a tomato as well. The wine was really yummy! It would have been around a $30 bottle of wine back home, if not more!

After our meal, we chatted with the owner of the hostel and they tried to find someone who spoke English in order to figure out what we needed. After a lot of charades, we let them know we needed a place to stay the next night and they ended up calling the next albergue for us. I have no idea how we managed to get them to do that. Neither one of us understood each other but they were so awesome in trying to help us and eventually calling the next day's albergue to reserve our spot. They also gave us the forms to send our packs ahead again.

We headed out around 8:00 p.m. to explore the town and head to Giacomo's dinner. We went to the store again and I bought another bottle of the wine we had enjoyed earlier. Diane bought an almond cake to share. The wine was so great that we wanted to share a bottle with Giacomo and his friends. We ran into the couple we had met in Reliegos. They were headed into the church for mass. We would have loved to have joined them, but we were headed to dinner, so we bid them farewell and continued on our path.

We found the albergue and went inside to find Giacomo. He was busy starting dinner and most of the others were out. We helped him

The Journey Inward

set up his dinner table for the large crew that he was expecting. We ended up with around 15 people at the table. He made a great pasta with onion, carrots, garlic, oil, wine, and tomatoes. We had awesome bread with it along with sliced tomatoes. It was a wonderful dinner. It was very different because most of the people did not speak English and many languages were used at the table. No matter the language barrier, we had a wonderful time with this large crowd of people who had adopted Giacomo and Angel as their pack leaders. They seemed to follow wherever they went and you couldn't ask for a better pair of gentlemen to follow! We ended dinner with the almond cake that Diane had brought. Then Diane and I helped clean up and wash dishes along with one of the other diners. Giacomo was thankful for the help and we were thankful for the wonderful dinner and friendship. We managed to find our way back to our hostel and to a good night's sleep.

Steps: 35,891

Portomarin – Palas de Rei

Day 28 of 31 (September 27th):
Kilometers: 25.2
Miles: 15.7

We decided to send our backpacks ahead again today, so we left them at the drop-off spot at the check-in desk. We wandered back into the town area and found a place to have some breakfast. As we started to head out for the day, I had to stop to fix my boots. Some days you could not get your boots just right. After walking all the way up the stairs the day before, we had to walk back down all those steps again to the bridge. As we got to the bridge, it was extremely foggy! The first part of the trip was through a nice wooded area.

We felt utterly exhausted on our walk. We could tell that our bodies were wearing down and we needed a break, but we were so close to the finish that we wanted to continue to press on. At this point, Diane said that she felt like she wanted to be DONE. She was missing the comforts of home.

The trek was not too overcrowded with the Camino newbies, so we were not as frustrated as the previous day. The route took us through many small towns, passing cows and cornfields along the way. We passed a family of five walking the Camino. A young couple in their 30's with three kids in tow...including one very small child being carried in a backpack carrier. It just made you wonder what their motivation was to make that trek with little ones along.

About an hour away from our destination, the fog finally cleared. We were thankful for that. When we got to Palas de Rei, we wandered a bit to find our albergue, Meson de Benito. The gentleman who checked us in spoke excellent English and was very nice. He gave us a tour of the place and led us to our beds. We took our showers and then went to find the laundry.

As our clothes were being washed and dried, we went to their restaurant and were able to order a pilgrims meal at 3:00. We were again very grateful for the early meal. While we were finishing our meal, one of the ladies who was waiting on us brought some more wine to our table. It was left over from the table next to us. After all this walking, we weren't going to turn down free wine!

After an early dinner, we went up to relax on our beds. The family of five ended up staying in our albergue which made the evening less quiet than desirable as the kids were left to run unchecked through the halls. Luckily, they were not in the same dorm room as us.

Diane spent a lot of time trying to research a place to stay for the next night. She let me know her frustrations with what she was finding. I could see that she was over-analyzing everything and eventually she became frustrated and decided to go to sleep. She told me to book anything that I found as I took over the research. I was frustrated with her over-analysis of the research and I began to look for a place to stay. I found a cool looking place and booked it via booking.com. I knew we also needed to find a place in Santiago and I researched hotels there as well. I found a nice, family-run hotel that was not far from the cathedral in Santiago. I decided to go ahead and book it without discussing it with Diane first. I knew we needed to reserve a place soon. I could see that Diane was starting to over-analyze every place she looked at, so I decided to make the bold move and guarantee a private room in Santiago. After booking both of those places, I too went to sleep early to try to recharge my body to make it through the last three days.

I had been in contact with Giacomo but was too tired to try to meet up with his group wherever they were headed for dinner. We could catch up tomorrow. Right now my body needed rest.

Steps: 33,921

Palas de Rei – Ribadiso

Day 29 of 31 (September 28th):
Kilometers: 25.8
Miles: 16.0

We ate breakfast at the café in our albergue and decided to send our backpacks ahead again today. We again were so exhausted that we just wanted to be able to make it to our destination. We went to find the appropriate forms to send the packs ahead. We set them out in front along with the others, trusting they would make it to our planned destination.

We came upon a town called Casanova and I messaged a picture of the town sign to Giacomo via WhatsApp. I told him it was a sign for him and Angel since they seemed to have a group of women pilgrims that seemed to be following along with them. A little later we found Eucalyptus trees. The forest of trees was very welcome after all of the desolate places we had walked during this trip.

We arrived in Ribadiso and passed two albergues next to the river and saw hikers soaking their feet in it. We were jealous and wished that we had decided to stay there. Just past there, we had to hike up a hill. We thought we had a lot further to go because our albergue said it was in Arzua. But just past these two albergues was our albergue for the night. As we approached it, we saw that they had a beautiful foot bath surrounded by seats with a fountain in the middle!

I was relieved that I managed to book an excellent albergue after all of the research that Diane had done the night before.

We quickly checked in, put our stuff on our bunks, and then came back out for a drink. We changed from our norm and we both ordered rum and diet cokes! We took our drinks to go soak our feet in the foot bath. Heaven! After twenty-nine days straight of walking, you cannot even imagine how good soaking our feet in this foot bath really was. At this point, it was better than sex!

We sat there as people came and went. We chatted with each person who came up to soak their feet. We got another round of rum and diet cokes and didn't want to go wash our clothes or take a shower. Therefore, we went totally against our normal routine and didn't do it! We sat there in our smelly clothes from the day's hike, got our third round of drinks, and continued to soak our feet in this incredible foot bath. By the time we were done with our drinks, we think we had met almost everybody staying in the albergue. We tried to get Giacomo and Angel to come up to join us but they stayed down at their albergue. I don't think they realized what they were missing with this incredible footbath!

While we were sitting there, we met a couple from Australia who had some pretty funny stories about their Camino. One story was about all the stuff he had left along the way including a pair of shorts that he desperately wanted later in their journey. Another was a day he went to pee off the trail. He leaned against an oak that broke and sent him plunging into a sewer-like river and he ended up rinsing off in one of the water urns that he found. The last story was where they split up walking and planned to meet up later. He didn't see her where he thought they would meet so he walked all the way back down a steep hill and still didn't see her. He walked back up the hill and finally found her after being totally exhausted from the extra miles. They vowed to plan a meeting spot for any future times that they split off. Diane and I laughed at all of their stories. They definitely had quite the adventure on this trip!

The Journey Inward

We finally got to the point where we were hungry and found out that we could order food at any time. We did not have to wait until 8:00 p.m. to order a pilgrim's menu. It was actually like a normal restaurant and they had plenty of great choices. As we waited for our food, Diane and I looked at different options for a hostel for the following day. I found one that had four beds and we thought it would be nice to have someone else stay with us to cut the cost for all three of us. We had met Suzanne three days earlier and knew that she was no longer walking with her previous walking partner, so I walked over to ask her if she would like to join us in that hostel the following evening. She thought that was a great idea too, so I gave her all the info on where we would be staying and I booked the room. We swapped phone numbers for us to keep in touch the next day so that she could walk on her own schedule and we could meet at the hostel that next afternoon.

Our dinner came and we both had wonderful meals along with more wine. That night we stayed in a room with six bunk beds and only one other one was occupied by another couple. The man was a very big man that Diane was sure would snore...he didn't. Diane woke up in the middle of the night and almost passed out when she got out of her bed. Apparently, the heat had been turned up and it was about 90 degrees in the room at 2:00 a.m. It was definitely not the norm as we were typically sleeping in layers and still a bit chilled. She found the thermostat and turned it down to a normal temperature.

Steps: 34,990

Ribadiso – Arca

Day 30 of 31 (September 29th):
Kilometers: 22.2
Miles: 13.8

We had our usual breakfast at the albergue. Our start was a gentle uphill climb into the town that we thought would be the destination from the day before. As we wandered through the town of Ribadiso, we came upon two ladies and an older gentleman. When we passed them, the gentleman pumped his fist in the air in a universal gesture that he was rooting for us! He didn't speak English, but we felt the love as he cheered us on. It was so sweet to get that support along The Way. It meant so much to us; it gave us energy and determination to finish our day and reach our ultimate destination!

Our walk was a fairly normal day. It wasn't too long and didn't have too many huge ascents or descents so it was a pleasant walk for the day. Diane and I chatted as we walked. It was our second to last day on the hike and our last evening before entering Santiago. We anticipated achieving our goal and the welcomed rest that we would have afterward. While we had read of many pilgrims who missed being on the Camino after arriving in Santiago, neither of us thought we would feel that way. We would be happy to be done hiking for a while!

The Journey Inward

We got to Arca and had to wander around town for a bit to find our hostel for the night. We checked in and the owner was wonderful! He showed us to a very nice room with four beds in it. We would only need three but it was a very warm, inviting room. The beds were cute with green and red plaid tops and green sides to the bedspread. Each of them had two towels for us and an extra pillow. He gave us detergent and a bucket to wash our clothes in the shower with us and then hang them out on the line. We were on the second floor so I was very careful about hanging my laundry out there. I didn't want a deja vu event of dropping my clothes to the ground where I couldn't retrieve them! Haha! As I wandered around the albergue, I noticed the owner was in the kitchen area ironing sheets. Who irons sheets these days?

You know you have been on the Camino too long when you are really impressed and feel spoiled because the ceiling fan has a remote control. Such luxury! While Diane was in the shower, I connected with Suzanne and helped her get to the hostel and to the room we were in once she got there. Very shortly after that, she showed up at our room. We gave her the info on showers and laundry and let her chill as I took a shower. She was next in the shower before we headed out to dinner together.

I checked in with Giacomo. They were staying in the same town but had not arrived yet. I asked where they were staying in Santiago and he texted me the albergue where they would be staying. It was close to our hostel, so I told him that we could catch up tomorrow after we both finished our hike.

We wandered through town until we found a nice restaurant to get our last pilgrims meal. As we passed through the tables to sit down, there was a very good-looking young guy that looked me in the eyes as I passed him and said seductively, "Buen Camino." Dang, that was a pleasant surprise! Diane looked at me with a look that said: "what was that about?" Shrugging my shoulders, I told her that I had no clue, but he sure was cute! Unfortunately, he smoked, so he was a bit more unattractive after I saw that, but his attention was greatly appreciated. He had still put a smile on my face. It got me thinking of opening myself up to dating again.

We had a very nice meal and Diane and I enjoyed getting to know Suzanne better. We were really happy to have her sharing our room and our wonderful dinner time. We had a great meal and then headed back to our hotel. We got ready for bed and our final day on the Camino! The anticipation was overwhelming. The next day we would reach our goal which would be a huge accomplishment. I am not sure how I got to sleep as I envisioned walking into Santiago!

Steps: 30,040

The Journey Inward

Arca – Santiago

Day 31 of 31 (September 30th):
Kilometers: 20.0
Miles: 12.4

Our walk was a fairly short walk compared to other days, but it seemed to take forever to get there. We had a very long walk uphill and the steep incline seemed to never end. I think it was just the anticipation of finally arriving in Santiago! This was the day! The day we had anticipated through many months of preparation and thirty-one straight days of walking. As I walked these final miles it was such a bittersweet feeling. We were about to complete not only our hike but a major bucket list item! While I was going to be glad to stop walking for a while, I was going to miss the joy of relaxing in the afternoon with a glass of sangria or red wine and then eating anything I wanted. Most of all I was going to miss the great friends that we had met on the Camino!

    A little after 10:00 a.m. we heard something behind us and I looked back to see our runners coming up behind us. These two guys had passed us the last several days on the trail. They were not walking the Camino; they were running the Camino! The first day they passed us, we were shocked to see them running. They were running the Camino! The second day we saw them we just found it very interesting to have them pass us again. The third day they passed us

I couldn't help but cheer them on, so I gave them a big woohoo as they passed us. They were in front of us when I did this and they turned around and ran backward for a brief second and pumped their fists in the air in victory. On the subsequent days, I always cheered them on when they passed us. On this final day, I saw them far enough behind us that I was able to grab my phone out of my fanny pack and take a picture of them as they were approaching us for the last time. They always had on matching shirts and this day they were wearing fluorescent orange shirts. In a final gesture, I cheered them on that last run. I wished we could have run into those two guys at one of our stops for the day because I would have loved to have heard their story!

Since we knew it was going to be a hectic time in Santiago, we decided to stop and eat lunch today even though we only had about an hour left to walk. We stopped at a little café and I had one of the best sandwiches that I had eaten on the Camino. It was pork, egg, and cheese on a magnificent crusty roll and was delicious! I considered ordering an extra one! They had wifi, so I put in their wifi password and I was able to connect to WhatsApp to check in there. I had received a voice message from Giacomo via WhatsApp and he told me they were twelve kilometers away and that we would get together for a huge party. He sent a big hug to us which in his accent sounded like "huge" which I thought was very endearing. He ended his message with "Buen Camino"! That was such a sweet thing to do! I loved this guy! How thoughtful!

We headed out of the café and continued our final trek. We were getting close and the anticipation increased. We came upon the airport. It was a very rude awakening after hiking in the peaceful areas for 31 days. We had such peaceful walks until now. We rarely listened to music, only one or two times. We were just used to the peacefulness of the hike. We really tuned into nature and the occasional conversation in passing with the other hikers along the way. Therefore, the sound of the airplanes was a symbol of getting back into the chaos of civilization and it was pretty harsh to accept!

The Journey Inward

To make matters worse, as we passed the airport, we also passed a huge area where they were cutting down trees. I have no idea why they were cutting down trees but you could hear the sound as they pushed the tree down and it fell to the ground. It was such a shock to the system. We were used to being in nature and appreciating all of the beauty of nature. To see and hear the awful process of them knocking down trees was very distressing!

A short walk later, we started to enter the city of Santiago. As we approached we got two thumbs up by a gentleman who saw us walk up to the city. A short while later we had another cheer from another gentleman. It was so impressive to have them cheer us on as we entered the city! What a thrill! That was on the outskirts. As we entered the city, it drastically changed. It was very weird! It was still a very long trudge to the cathedral. After the welcome from the two gentlemen outside of the city, we expected a little more excitement as we entered the city. We got just the opposite. As we walked through the city, people did not acknowledge us. Everyone turned the other way and completely ignored us, which is completely opposite from all of the other towns along the way of the Camino.

As we walked into the city, I realized how large a city it really was. I began feeling sorry for myself as we neared the cathedral. I really wanted to see our Swedish couple, but I had no way of getting in touch with them. I knew that in a city this size it would be impossible to find them. I was starting to get very upset that we would end here and not be able to see our dear friends again. We came upon a split in the road and took the wrong turn, so we backtracked to get back on the trail. We began getting really close to the cathedral. We passed through a plaza where a few roads met and figured out our correct route to the cathedral. As we walked down this route, guess who we ran into? Yes, our Swedish couple along with their companion from Taiwan! I broke down in tears when I told them that I didn't think we would end up seeing them here. They asked when we had arrived and we said that we hadn't arrived yet. We still had not made it to the cathedral! It was so very sweet to see them as we approached our final stop! Again, the wonderful miracle of running into our dear friends occurred at just the right moment! The Camino magic happened again!

After chatting with them, we continued the final couple of blocks to the cathedral. We finally made it to the cathedral! Part of it was wrapped in scaffolding but it was still a beautiful sight! It was beyond my imagination to finally be standing in front of the cathedral. The realization of our accomplishment was starting to sink in. We actually did it! We took the obligatory pictures of our backpacks over our heads as we celebrated our accomplishment! Diane also posed sideways with both arms in a fist pose, one in front and one behind…a victory he-man stance. I had to laugh at her one more time. I loved this girl!

We then headed around the corner to figure out where the office was to get our Compostelas. We found it and started to stand in the long line. As we were standing there, we noticed a guy who was taking groups back to their office to check them in there. It was groups of three or more. We ran into a guy from California who we had met earlier on our hike and had chatted with many times. He was from the United States, so we formed a group of three. When the guy came back out, we chatted with him and introduced him to our "group" from the US and we got invited to get the Compostela through him instead of waiting in line. He ushered us out to the office next door and gathered all of our information. He asked each of us if we wanted a second certificate noting the distance, which we all three wanted, of course. Once he got that, he told us to give him about an hour and then to check back in with him.

We headed out to find a bar to grab a drink! We found a place with outdoor seating so we all ordered a drink and relaxed. We celebrated our victory! We made it to Santiago! The hour went quickly and we headed back to pick up our Compostelas. While we waited in their office to get our Compostelas, we noticed that they also had the tubes available for purchase for storing our Compostelas safely for our journey back home. Then it was finally time; we were each given the coveted document that proved that you made the walk! What a sweet feeling to be handed that document! We had now "officially" hiked the Camino.

We headed out to find our hostel for the night. On our way to the hostel, who do you think we ran into? Yes, it was Giacomo and Angel! They were on their way to the cathedral when we ran into them on our way to find our hostel. How cool is that! In fact, we met them in the same spot that we came across the Swedish couple when we were on our way to the cathedral.

We managed to find our hostel. We entered it and felt comforted that it would be a pleasant place. It was a lovely family run hostel and the owner's son spoke English so it was a very easy check-in process. While checking in, we saw a flyer for a bus trip that left the next day and visited Finisterre, Muxia and one of their amazing waterfalls. When we said we were interested, he called the company and booked us for the trip. He gave us instructions on how to meet up with this bus, along with many suggestions for dinner and nightlife. We headed to the elevator and it was so small that we both couldn't fit in there with the backpacks. We laughed as we put both backpacks in. I stayed with the packs; Diane took the stairs and met me when I arrived at our floor.

After washing our clothes in the sink and hanging them to dry on our balcony, we headed back out to relax and have a drink. We went back to the same little plaza area where we originally were lost heading to the cathedral. As we walked through this plaza, guess who we saw again! Our beautiful Swedish couple! We were so extremely excited to see them again for another drink that we immediately sat down to join them!

They were sitting with a man from India so we instantly got involved with their conversation learning more about this interesting guy. They were already sipping red wine which they said was very good, so we ordered a bottle of the same thing. I guess we should have looked at a wine menu. We ended up paying 15 Euro for that bottle of wine. Heck, that was twice as much as the cost of some of our albergues along the way! It was good, but not worth that much. It was sticker shock after paying as little as 1 Euro for a nice glass of wine and paying 8 Euros for a very nice bottle of wine at the market! We had become so spoiled with the smaller towns on the Camino! We had to get back to our big town mode and start looking at prices.

Thankfully, they brought out free tapas so we were able to have a snack before dinner. We had contacted Giacomo and he finally came out to join us along with one of the girls who had been walking with their entourage. We had dinner with her previously and she was so cute and sweet! After we were done with our wine, Giacomo's crew finally got together and were ready for dinner. We joined them at a nearby restaurant. Even with the big crowd, Giacomo ended up sitting next to me which I was happy to see. He helped me with the menu as it was in Spanish.

I ended up with a first course of soup, a second course of chicken steak, and then flan for dessert that was actually pretty good! Giacomo ordered some wine and shared with us. It was a wonderful celebratory dinner with their sweet walking group. We had a fun time at the dinner even though their service was very slow! When we were done, we walked out and chatted outside for a bit. We didn't know if we would see Giacomo again because he was going to continue walking on to Finisterre, so we gave him a big hug and told him to have a safe trip!

As we sat back in our room for the night, I chatted with the guy back in Charleston whom I had chatted with earlier in the trip. When I told him that I finally made it to Santiago, he made the comment that it was easy. I told him it wasn't easy at all! Nobody back home had any idea as to how hard this trip really was! They didn't know the excruciating pain that I had endured every day with my knee. They didn't understand that every day was a mental exercise to keep my legs moving in the right direction while the rest of my body screamed at me. I FINALLY MADE IT!!! I was so ecstatic! There were a lot of people who had been following my progress, but they didn't know the struggles that I had gone through to accomplish this. This guy's comment put it all into perspective that everyone had virtually hiked along with me to see the fun we had, but they didn't have any idea on how hard the hike really was. I guess I didn't share the pain I had as often that I felt it, so they would know how really difficult it was. I set my frustration aside, snuggled in my bed and relished in the thought that I didn't have to walk the next day. We would be taking a bus to Muxia and Finisterre in the morning.

Steps: 32,592

Janet Charbonneau

Muxia and Finisterre

October 1st:

We woke up early to catch our bus for the final section of the Camino. We wanted to experience Muxia and Finisterre but did not want to hike there. Our bus allowed us to visit both within a day. We were excited to be able to become a tourist and sit back to relax as the bus drove us there. We first stopped in Muxia. Our bus took us through the quaint little town and stopped at the church about a mile out of town. I was disappointed that we didn't get to explore the town, but I fell in love with the huge rocks near the church. The views near the church were breathtaking, with the waves of the Atlantic crashing on the rocks below. The church was not open, but we got to take a sneak peek into it through the bars over the doors.

We also stopped in Finisterre, where we got to see the lighthouse and stop at the mile marker 0. I asked Diane to take a picture of me in front of that marker. We wandered around and went to visit the boulders that overlooked the ocean. There was a gentleman playing the bagpipes as we walked over to the lighthouse. After exploring the area, the bus dropped us off in town to have lunch. The town sat overlooking the water and we found a nice lunch spot where we could see the brightly painted fishing boats in the harbor. I ordered shrimp for lunch and received a plate of nine huge shrimp with their heads still on them. They were artfully displayed with their heads pointed to the center of the plate with their bodies stretched out like spokes on a wheel. I was not used to having shrimp served with their heads on them, so it was a little surprising. They were delicious!

On our way back to Santiago, we got a chance to stop by to visit the Ezaro waterfall which tumbles down huge rocks and lands in the Atlantic Ocean. The waterfall was beautiful and we were grateful to be able to stop there on our way back to Santiago. Our bus passed by the long enticing sand beach in Carnota and made a stop to see the largest Horreo in Spain. A Horreo is a building set on top of pillars to keep rodents away from the crops inside. This one was from the 18th-century and made of stone. It was quite interesting. As we rode back to Santiago, I fell asleep in my seat, happy to be able to relax on the trip instead of walking.

Santiago

October 2nd:

We slept in a bit and then grabbed a bite at the bar in our hotel. We headed out to explore the Santiago Cathedral and attend the pilgrims mass at noon. The mass was so crowded that we found a place to sit on some steps off to the right side. The mass was said in Latin, so it was hard to follow, but definitely a wonderful experience. We were fortunate enough to be able to see the botafumeiro swing during the mass. It is a metal container that contains incense and is swung from a rope suspended from the dome in the roof of the cathedral. A pulley mechanism is used by eight men in red robes to swing the botafumeiro. They say it can swing in a 65-meter (approximately 213-foot) arc and reaches speeds up to 80 kph (just under 50 mph). It was a very impressive sight! They do not swing the botafumeiro at every mass so we were very grateful to be able to see it.

After mass was over, we went outside to let the crowds exit the church. We viewed the ornate details on the outside of the church. Nearby, there was a man dressed all in white and even had his skin painted white so he looked like a statue of Ghandi. He was standing as still as a statue but as you approached him he would hand you a tiny piece of paper rolled up like a scroll. The paper he handed me said: "Nadie tiene tanta necesidad de una sonrisa como el que no se la puede dar a los demás" which translates to "Nobody is so much in need of a smile that he cannot give it to others." What a nice thought!

The Journey Inward

We continued wandering around and ended up in the gift shop of the cathedral. I bought a blessed rosary for my Mom which I thought she would enjoy since she was Catholic. Soon the crowds had subsided and we walked back into the cathedral to look around it. This was the ultimate destination to visit the burial place of St. James. The altar was extremely ornate and had a statue of St. James overlooking it. We climbed the staircase behind the altar and were able to rest our hand on his shoulders and whisper a message of thanks. Next, we went down into the crypt that contained St. James' bones. We walked through the rest of the church admiring the intricate details throughout.

After visiting the cathedral, we wandered through some of the shops heading back towards our hotel. Diane went looking for some shoes and she stopped in one of the shops to try some on. Instead of little socks made of pantyhose material, they gave her two clear plastic bags to put on her feet when she tried them on. I laughed as she put the plastic bags on her feet and then tried on the new shoes with the large plastic bags sticking out from them. I went to another shop after seeing a square piece of blue pottery with a scalloped shell in the middle. I love collecting pottery and blue was my favorite pottery color. This piece had the symbol of the Camino on it and it would be the perfect souvenir for this trip. I asked them to get it out of the display window. I fell in love with it! It would be a wonderful reminder of my Camino. It was the only one they had in the store. I purchased it and asked them to pack it safely to be able to handle the flight back to Charleston.

On our way back to the hotel, we found a quaint little bar called La Flor. We managed to get a small table in the back and enjoyed watching the wait staff and the patrons. The food was awesome! I ordered chicken fajitas, which came out already assembled, but they were delicious! Had we stayed another day, we would have definitely gone back for another meal. It was an excellent restaurant!

Santiago – Madrid

October 3rd:

We found that we could fly to Madrid quicker than getting there by train, so we had booked a flight before we left for Spain. We took a bus to the airport and checked in for our flight. It was a fairly quick flight and we were soon in Madrid for our last day in Spain. We hailed a taxi that took us to our hotel, which Diane had also booked before we left for Spain. We had decided to splurge on a nice hotel room that was within walking distance from many attractions in Madrid. After a luxurious bath for each of us, we went out to explore the city.

We walked a couple of blocks and found a place for a bite to eat. We then set out to wander the streets of Madrid. We saw a cool chariot and horses statue at the top of a building. We wandered into a few shops, including a candy shop, and then found ourselves in front of the Royal Palace. Feeling tired, we turned around to head back to our hotel. We stopped at a little outdoor café and ordered a pitcher of sangrias. As we walked back, we ran across a few people that were dressed in one color and posing as statues, so we stopped to watch them for a while. We then headed back towards our hotel, hoping to find a place to eat dinner.

Upon arriving at our hotel, we still had not run across any restaurants, so we wandered up to another street. We found a few restaurants and started to look at menus to decide where we wanted to go. We looked at the menu and liked the SOHO Bar and Restaurant, but they had a wait for a table, so we decided to wait at the bar. There was a really cute bartender with dark hair and a scruff of a mustache and beard who waited on us. He introduced himself as Alexander. We looked at the drink menu and both ordered a tropical drink. We chatted with our bartender as he waited on us. He was very attentive and we enjoyed our banter back and forth. Our table became available and we decided to just stay at the bar and order dinner. These two single women could not pass up an extremely sexy bartender waiting on us! We looked at the drink menu again and ordered another round of drinks. We eventually looked at the dinner menu and ordered dinner. I had enjoyed my chicken fajitas so much the night before that I ordered chicken and steak fajitas.

As we waited for dinner, our bartender came over with free shots for us. They were shots of Canadian whiskey and cinnamon. I asked to see the bottle and it was called Thunder Bitch. How appropriate for these two single women who just conquered the Camino! We finished dinner and ordered another round of drinks before heading back to the hotel.

As we left the restaurant, we started to walk back to the hotel and Diane wanted to walk one way and I another. I told her that I definitely remembered the way that we got there, so we followed my route back to the hotel. Thankfully, I was correct with my memory. While Diane was awesome at routing us through the entire Camino, she wasn't so great after a few rounds of drinks. We laughed as we entered our hotel, thankful to have made it back safely. It would be astonishing if we made our flight the next day after all those drinks, but we had an excellent last night in Spain!

Madrid – Charleston

October 4th:

We managed to get up, get packed and request a taxi to take us to the airport. We checked in and got to the terminal with no issues. We were on the same flight to Atlanta but in different rows. It was a bittersweet flight since I had to go to work the next day and it was so different being off the Camino. I was looking forward to getting home but knew it would be hard to get back into the same old routine since I had changed on this journey.

After getting to Atlanta and going through the entire customs process, I found Diane waiting for me at the entrance to the SkyTrain which would take us to our terminals. We were on different flights at different terminals, so this would be our last point together. We hugged and said our goodbyes, but we knew we would continue this friendship that had been bonded on the Camino.

I was hoping that my flight to Charleston would be on time. There had been a threat of a hurricane coming near Charleston. It, along with a stalled front and a low-pressure system off the coast, had produced 15-20 inches of rain in the Charleston area with some areas getting 25 inches. There was flooding throughout Charleston and I was not sure that I could get to my house, even if I could get to Charleston.

The Journey Inward

Since our flight had arrived early in Atlanta, I had no problem getting to my connecting flight to Charleston. It was on time, so I knew I could at least get to Charleston. I had to pray that I could get home from there. Once I arrived in Charleston, I texted my friend, Pam, who was coming to pick me up. She had to detour in order to get to the airport because of the flooding in her area. She finally managed to get to the airport and pick me up. I had stored my purse and personal laptop in my desk at my company's office, so I asked if she thought we could get there. Those roads had flooded during a much lesser storm, so I was doubtful. We decided to give it a try.

She drove to the office with no flooding issues getting there. Then we both realized we didn't have a card key to get into the door after hours. Mine was in my wallet inside the office and she didn't have hers with her. She was the manager of the building and had a spare key hidden so we finally managed to get into the building. My keys had been stored in her car, so I was able to get into my office. After getting my purse and laptop, we headed to my house. One of the roads to my house had been flooded earlier in the day. I was grateful that the waters had subsided and we were able to make it to my house.

We entered my subdivision and it was very dark. It appeared that the electricity was out in our subdivision. We got to my house and I went inside. The electricity was indeed out, but it was so nice to be home! Pam invited me to stay at her house, but I was just so glad to be home that I didn't want to leave again. Besides, I needed to go to work the next day and didn't want to pack everything for work. I decided to stay there since I had plenty of candles and flashlights. I had been through hurricanes before and was familiar with surviving without electricity. Thankfully, after a couple of hours, the electricity came on and I could finally enjoy the comforts of home sweet home!

Epilogue

They say that hiking the Camino is life changing. Sometimes you expect to get the big "Aha" moment in the middle of the Camino, but most people do not get that. They get the real meaning of their hike many months after they finish their hike. My Camino has continued to grow within me, so, even three years later, I continue to get those "aha" moments.

My first "Aha" moment was that I actually accomplished my goal. I had hiked the Camino de Santiago! My total number of steps for the hike was 1,005,294. I had walked over a million steps throughout this journey! I could check off another big item on my bucket list. That was huge! And I had done it after my divorce. It was very symbolic to move on and travel after my divorce.

When I was done with the hike, I was just so glad to be done with the daily walking! It was very grueling to my body and my knees were ready for a break! The first couple of days that we were done, it felt really weird to not be trekking out on the Camino. On the one day that we took a bus to Finisterre and Muxia, we were so grateful to be riding on the bus and finally being tourists instead of hiking that entire way. It felt so amazing to sit on a bus and relax (and sleep) on the way to our next destination. We did manage to walk around Madrid the day before we flew back home, but I have to admit I tired easily! While chatting with the bartender during our last dinner in Spain, I realized that I was interested in trying to date again. I was really attracted to him and realized that I indeed wanted to find the right guy for a serious relationship. I had been so tired from the daily walking on the Camino that I had not thought about dating but the bartender got me thinking otherwise!

It was very difficult to fly back to the United States on a Sunday and start work again on a Monday. I had no time to decompress. I missed my work team who were all very good friends of mine and I was looking forward to going to work. It was just such a shock to go from the daily hiking back to the daily grind of work. Since there had been so much flooding, I learned that we had the option to work from home on Monday. Unfortunately, I had left my work laptop in my desk on the project site while I was hiking the Camino. I felt it would be safer there. Therefore, I had to go into the project office that Monday, so I could retrieve my laptop. Thankfully it was very quiet, so I was able to weed through my 200 emails and get organized and back into the routine before I saw many people.

The next day I was welcomed back by all my dear coworkers and I felt the true friendship that I had with them. I realized how special it was to work with a team that was more like a family. The best part of that day was proving to everybody that I actually accomplished my hike! It was especially sweet to prove my determination for finishing for the ones I knew had doubted that I would complete the hike.

As I settled back into the normal routine, I started to look at my life. I was proud to be able to check off one more bucket list item! That accomplishment reminded me of how I used to be before my divorce; back then I was always ready to take on new challenges. I realized that I needed to make some changes to my daily life.

While talking to people about my journey, I became aware that, even though I had shared my experiences on Facebook, I had not shared my true self with my friends and family. Since I am usually not one to complain, I mentioned my knee being painful, but I did not continue to share the struggle that I had with it. I had extreme pain on a daily basis and I kept this to myself instead of sharing it.

I also didn't let people know how much their likes and comments on Facebook meant to me. I didn't ask for their encouragement when I was struggling and needed it the most. I was using the support from my friends to help me make it through each day, but I didn't let everyone know how much it meant to me. Therefore, I wasn't getting as much encouragement as I would have if only I had shared my need to them. I discovered that I needed to be vulnerable and show my true feelings. I needed to let everyone know how much their encouragement meant to me.

One thing I recognized during my hike via the support that I got on my Facebook posts was how dear my Charleston friend network was. They had been more supportive during my hike than my family had been. I felt like they were part of my "extended family." I finally realized that Charleston was my home. It was the first time since I had moved to Charleston that it actually felt like home.

As I settled back into my life after the Camino, I realized that I needed to ask for help and support when I was struggling. I had a huge community of friends and family around the country and around the world that was there for me. I just had to learn to ask for it when I desired it and to accept it when they gave it to me. While it made me feel very vulnerable to ask, it is what I needed to do to open myself up to the love and support that was available to me.

I relied on this support as I worked on writing and publishing this book. My friends and family have been there to cheer me on. Several of them also gratuitously volunteered to review my book for grammar and content. I am grateful for all the support I received!

I had been afraid to make any type of commitment in my life since my divorce. After having lost a job and barely being able to pay my bills, I had feared making a commitment to owning a dog, even though I really wanted to get another Golden Retriever. I was scared that I would not be able to afford to take care of him/her. I was apprehensive about committing to a relationship as well. I believe that was keeping me from finding the right person for me. Therefore, I was home alone with no dog and no promise of a boyfriend either.

The Journey Inward

I finally got over the fear of owning a dog and decided to adopt another Golden. Once I had made that decision, I leaped in quickly by putting in adoption applications to many different Golden rescue organizations within a few hours' drive. I worked with one of the organizations in Atlanta but it did not look promising since they only wanted to place their dogs with someone who worked from home or was a stay at home Mom. How many people fit into that category? I had been a wonderful Dog-Mom to Max and Bailey for years, but that didn't help. I thought the requirement of being home most of the day and not allowing you to work full-time away from home was totally ridiculous! Like having a full-time job and taking care of your dog was not possible?

I contacted another local organization, Grateful Goldens Rescue of the Low Country, that didn't have such a ludicrous rule. They were based in South Carolina with volunteers and foster families in Charleston.

I submitted my application and then was contacted for a house visit so they could verify that it was a safe house for one of their Goldens. The visit went very well and their volunteer said they saw no reason that I wouldn't qualify to be able to adopt a dog. They did warn me that it might take many months or a year to get a dog, so I set my expectations for that timeframe.

A few weeks went by after the home visit and I sent them an email for a status to see if I was eligible for a Golden. They responded by telling me to check out Holly on their website and that I could meet her at an event in Florence, South Carolina. In my mind, I had wanted a male Golden, but I decided to take a look at her profile. Holly had the dark Golden color like my last two Goldens and she was around 80 pounds. She had all the qualities I was looking for in a Golden, so I was excited to meet her.

The next weekend, I drove the two hours up to Florence to visit Holly and she was extremely shy at the event. George, the coordinator, allowed me to take her for a walk and it wasn't a very good walk. She pulled a lot and had no clue how to walk on a leash, but she was very sweet and I had a good feeling about her. I sat with her at the event for a couple of hours and took her on another walk. I was growing attached to her.

She had been a breeder's dog up in Myrtle Beach, SC. The breeder had moved to upstate South Carolina and had left Holly, her sister, and another dog behind. The neighbor knew that he had moved, realized his three dogs had been left behind and contacted a local rescue group. That organization contacted Grateful Goldens and they brought Holly into their organization for adoption.

In December 2015 I decided to foster Holly to see how she would do. She was extremely shy and, the first weekend she was with me, she would not even come near me. I could tell that she had been abused and was afraid of people. I sat down and cried that weekend; it was incomprehensible to me that someone could do that to a dog!

It was not the first time that I had to rehabilitate an abused dog. I had been a volunteer with a service dog organization that placed service dogs with Veterans. I had taken one of their service dogs out for socialization many weekends before he was placed with his Veteran. He had been such a goofy, sweet pup and I knew I would miss him when he got placed. After a few weeks with his Veteran, the Veteran reported weird actions by this dog and they contacted me to see if I had seen any of those actions. I had not and I instantly knew there was something wrong.

After that organization did a house visit with the Veteran, the service dog was pulled out and I was asked to foster him. The minute I saw him I knew he had been abused. He was literally just a shell. His goofy personality was gone and his eyes had a vacant look. I was heart-broken! I fostered him for several months. He was with me twenty-four hours a day and went everywhere with me. I was grateful that my workplace allowed me to take this service dog into work with me every day. After heaping tons of love on him, I was able to get him back to being a happy dog. He never did get back to his old, goofy self, but I could see that he was doing well. He got placed with a new Veteran and ended up with a wonderful life having fun helping his new Veteran. It was great to see pictures of the great places that he and his Veteran had visited together.

I had hoped to train my new dog to be a therapy dog to be able to visit nursing homes and hospitals. I wondered if Holly would be able to pull out of her shell and start socializing. After a couple of months, I could see that she was slowly making progress. I fell in love with her and adopted her in February 2016! I had made the commitment which felt very extreme for me! I had a dog that was dependent on me. Still being single, it was very stressful, but I felt confident that I would be able to support her.

After three years with Holly, she has made wonderful progress. She is much more sociable with people, but I don't think she would do well as a therapy dog. I love her dearly though. She has brought much joy to my life. She is the first female dog that I have owned; she prances around sometimes in a girly prance, so I nicknamed her "Miss Priss." She adores rolling in the grass in her backyard. She loves to lay on her back with her front paws straight up in the air asking for tummy rubs, while she shows me a silly, toothy grin with her fangs sticking out. That is how she usually greets me in the morning when I wake up, so I start most days with a laugh from her silliness. She is a sweet, goofy pup and she makes me laugh all the time! Every time I feed her, she sits patiently and nudges my arm like she is thanking me for her meal. She follows me around the house and always wants to be next to me. She is peacefully sleeping nearby on one of her many dog beds as I write this. I am very grateful that we rescued each other!

Commitment to a Goldie was just the first of many changes that I made when I returned. I also decided to take the plunge and buy the house I was living in. I knew I needed to wait until my credit report was in a state where I could qualify for the house. What I didn't know was if I actually could qualify for the house. I took the huge step forward and talked to my friend who was a real estate agent and he recommended a mortgage broker. I then worked with her to see how much I needed as a down payment and what I needed on my credit report. I needed to have a couple of negative credit card statuses fall off of my credit report which were scheduled to be done by January 2017.

I was ecstatic! I now had a plan for saving for a down payment and knowing when my credit report would work for me to buy this house. I was really excited to have set this goal! A year later I had achieved the goals for buying my house and, in February 2017, I had signed all the paperwork. I had purchased my house! I was so grateful for being able to own my house by myself. I had overcome another fear and made the commitment of a house. I've had fun being able to redecorate the house now that it is actually mine. I sit on the back deck often, listening to the crickets, cicadas and tree frogs and am grateful to live in this peaceful spot. I sat here today smiling as I watched my neighbors walk by in this wonderful, friendly neighborhood and am so happy to be able to live in such an awesome place.

Having made the commitments to own a dog and a house, I wanted to release one more fear of commitment and decided to give the online dating thing another chance. I believe in the Law of Attraction; essentially it states that "like attracts like." What you think about, you bring about. I came to the realization that I was sabotaging my dating life. Prior to walking the Camino, I had been working on a book about our motorcycle trip and I believed that I really needed to finish the book before starting to date someone seriously. After returning from the Camino, I started writing this book. I continued to think that if I started dating someone then they would consume all my time and I would not get my book completed. I kept thinking that dating would sabotage the completion of either book and that thought was causing me to not be successful in dating. What I didn't realize was that, if I found the right man, then he would support my writing and give me time to finish the books.

With this newfound understanding, I continued with the online dating. My first few dates were the disasters like prior times, but then I had a few good first dates with just no chemistry. I managed to go on three dates with one guy but we just didn't match personality wise.

The Journey Inward

I was hearing a pattern where he would complain about his day and then at the very end would try to put a positive spin on it. But the one minute of positive endings was not masking the fifteen minutes of prior complaints. I needed someone who aligned with my positive attitude and his negativity was dragging me down.

With persistence, I found someone who was positive, had most of the qualities that I found valuable and gave me time to work on my book. While I thought he was being considerate and giving me time to work on my book, I came to realize that he just wasn't really into me. I deserved someone who treated me right and he wasn't it. I broke up with him and decided to move on.

Shortly after we broke up, I went on a first date with a guy who I really liked. Too many family and holiday obligations got in the way, so we never made it to the second date. I was disappointed because I was attracted to him, but he never asked me on a second date. At that point, I was frustrated with the difficulties of dating, so I shut myself down again to the dating process.

After a year and a half of staying out of the dating scene, I felt that I was finally ready to try again. Ironically I ran across the profile of the last guy I had gone out with. It was his profile in the same dating app where we had originally connected. While he had never asked me out on that second date, he had told me that he was interested, so I thought I would give it a chance and see if I could get that second date. I emailed him and crossed my fingers. I found out that he had been switched to third shift where he was working and the strange hours were taking a toll on him. He hadn't been able to date while working that shift. He said he had just changed jobs and was working first shift again. My timing had been perfect. After communicating for a few days, we made it to the second date, a movie followed by dinner. We had a fun time and I thought that we would continue to date, but after a couple days of texting, he quit communicating. I was really disappointed because I thought it was a good sign that after a year and a half he was still interested in going out. Frustrated and confused, I moved on.

As I started looking through the online dating apps again, I did some soul searching. While I thought I had opened myself up to dating again, I realized that deep down inside of me I was still scared of dating because I felt I needed to publish my book first. Even though my actions were saying I was ready to date, in my heart I still believed that dating would sabotage my chances of finishing my book. Therefore, I was attracting the wrong type of guys. I wanted to find a guy who was ready for a real relationship, not just a fling; someone who was honest, caring, and had a sense of humor. If they were thoughtful enough to send a text or leave a note saying they were thinking of me, then that was a big plus. I also loved when a guy was handy around the house or liked to cook.

My Camino spoke to me again and gave me the courage to really open my heart in order to attract the right type of guy. The right one would be there by my side to support me. He would be my cheerleader and encourage me to finish it. How did I not understand that concept for so long? How had I been too afraid that a guy would deter me from my dreams and goals? I should have known that the right guy would support me and my goals.

I was truly ready to be open to a relationship. I opened my mind and heart up to the possibility of finding a true, meaningful relationship, so I started looking through the dating app again and sending emails. Now that I had really opened myself up, I got a response from a guy who not only was extremely attractive, but his profile said he enjoyed the simple things in life. It said that he valued the little things, such as a compliment or sending a text just to say he was thinking of you. That was one of my valued qualities! The rest of the qualities that were in his profile aligned with the qualities that I wanted in a guy, so I was happy that he responded to my email.

Just after we started chatting, I left to visit my Mom over the July 4th holiday for a week and a half. We hadn't gotten a chance to meet yet, but we continued very deep text conversations and I knew he was exactly the type of guy that I was looking for. During our text conversation one evening, I told him that I had been thinking of one part of my book and that I needed to go edit that one section while I was feeling passionate about it. He agreed that I needed to work on it while it was passionately on my mind and told me to go make those edits. This was the type of support I needed; someone who encouraged me to write.

After I was finished, I texted him back. One of his comments was about the book being a number one seller. My comment back was that I needed to work on a marketing plan and that was going to be harder to write than the book was. His comment back was "Haha, I do marketing, you got this." I burst out laughing when I read that because I forgot that he was in marketing. I asked him to help me with my marketing plan and he agreed.

I went to sleep thinking of that marketing plan. I woke up at 3:30 in the morning and his words echoed in my head. I realized that the Camino magic had cast its spell on me again. I had been worried that dating would hinder my writing time and sabotage my ability to publish my book. What I had never considered was the possibility that a guy could help me with my book by helping me tackle the marketing piece of the process; it was an area where I lacked experience. It provided a possibility of bonding by working together as a team for one goal.

As I lay there in bed, my anxiety about dating disappeared. I realized that I just needed to open myself up to dating experiences and ones like this would appear. I discovered that if I kept myself open to all possibilities with no expectations, then I would receive more than I could ever imagine! As long as I stayed focused on my end goal of publishing this book while looking for the right guy, then the right guy would eventually find his way to me. I looked forward to experiencing my happily ever after!

When I returned to Charleston, we finally went on a first date, which I felt went very well. We continued to text after that and he agreed to also help me with my website. We decided that he needed to read my book so that he could help me with the marketing of it. I emailed it to him and he started reading it the next day. After a few more days of texting, he ended up ghosting me. That is a term used when someone just stops communicating with you. I thought we had a good first date, so had no idea why he disappeared. I thought maybe he didn't like the book and didn't want to have to try to market it. I laughed at that thought. I was pretty sure that wasn't the reason. Having gotten used to ghosting with online dating, I, at least, realized that he taught me that a guy can help me with my book publishing journey and can, at a minimum, be supportive to me. Therefore, I decided to continue with online dating and not get scared again.

I am still in the process, but am very open to dating and knowing the right guy will be cheering my progress. When I find that, then I know he could be the one. I am currently dating someone who has been very supportive of my writing. He understands my need to have the time to write and publish the book and he continues to cheer me on when I get stressed out over all the things that are involved with publishing a book. I am hoping that this relationship works out, but, if not, then I know that I need to remain open to love and I will definitely find my happily ever after!

Not only was my personal life going through many changes, but my job was as well. I was pulled off the project I had been working on for four years and I helped with business development for my company. Eventually, I was assigned to a new project. After being on the project for one month, I was assigned as the Account Manager for that project and another project in the same building. I was thrown into many situations where I was way beyond my comfort zone. I had to bring on two new employees and handle many uncomfortable personnel issues. I had never wanted to be a manager, so this was very stressful for me.

During my walk on the Camino, I had purchased a bracelet for only a few Euros. It just consisted of bright pink rope with a pewter scalloped shell on it. I never took it off and it was a symbol of the Camino for me. It reminded me that I had enough strength and determination to be able to finish the Camino, so there was nothing that I could not accomplish. I spent many times in my new position at work relying on that bracelet to give me the courage to accomplish my job. I often sat in my team lead meetings rubbing the scalloped shell on my bracelet as a reminder that I had the strength to be able to represent my team well.

Two and a half years after coming back from the Camino, I was sitting at work one day and realized that I had lost the pewter scalloped shell on my bracelet. The rope bracelet was still on my wrist, but the shell was gone. I was devastated. It was my daily reminder of my Camino and my inner strength.

I walked around a bit to see if I could find it, but I knew that it was pretty hopeless. This had been a day where I had walked around a tremendous amount. The warehouse where my work cube resided was very noisy that day and I had been on several phone calls. To get some quiet time for those calls, I had wandered around outside in the huge parking lot the size of a football field, constantly pacing as I talked. I was very skeptical that I would find it.

I sat at home that evening and realized that I was being sad about the loss of my bracelet for no logical reason. While I used the bracelet for reminding me of my inner strength, I actually had that strength inside me already. I didn't need a daily reminder that it was in there. I didn't lose the strength because I lost the shell. I realized it was my strength and courage that I could rely on any time I needed it. I felt much better about it.

A couple of days later I was sitting on my futon working on this book when I got up to fill my water glass. I came back to work on my book and looked down on the futon. What was sitting on my seat where I was just sitting a few minutes before? It hadn't been there when I sat down earlier; I was sure of that. I looked closer and it was my pewter scalloped shell from my bracelet. The Camino magic was back. How had it just miraculously appeared? I thought I had lost it at work. It had been a few days and several clothes changes later to just be caught in clothing. I was so happy to have my shell back! I had removed my bracelet from my wrist when I lost the shell; I decided not to put the shell back on the bracelet and back onto my wrist. Instead, I put it safely in my jewelry box as a memento of my journey of a lifetime. I knew my strength, courage, and determination was inside of me.

It took me a while to talk to Blaine about my resentments of him not taking the debt seriously and paying down my credit card. It was just a hard conversation to have over the phone. He eventually moved back to Charleston and I was able to see him face to face. Over dinner one evening, I explained my feelings about the debt and how I resented that he was not taking it seriously. It was a long discussion, but he finally understood that it was eating away at me. He agreed that he had not put much effort into paying it off because it was not important to him. He realized how much it meant to me, so he said he would work on paying off the card and has continued to do so.

With that burden released and having him nearby again, we started chatting more often and going out to dinner once in a while. Our friendship has blossomed as platonic friends. We are both supportive of each other's dating. We realized that we just weren't able to make the marriage work, but that we still had an awesome friendship. Blaine has been great in helping me with the remodeling of my house: painting, installing a ceiling fan, replacing bathroom fixtures, etc. He has also been very supportive of my book publishing process, helping push me forward when the fear of the process would stall me. I am grateful that we have been able to survive a divorce and come away as dear friends.

Some of my friendships have continued since the Camino. I am still friends with Diane and we have kept in touch mainly via Facebook. After all of her failed dating stories, she finally found the right guy. He moved to Arizona shortly after they started dating and she ended up moving from Wisconsin to Arizona to be with him. She used her Camino strength to quit her job, find a new one near him, sell her house, and make that scary move. Her Camino taught her to take the chance. She and her new boyfriend look like they are having a great time together. I am very happy for her and, since she met him via an online dating app, it gives me hope that the online dating process works.

I had emailed my sweet Swedish friends a couple of times after I returned but didn't end up staying in touch. I am sure after I publish this book that I will contact them for their address and send them a copy. They were such a special part of my Camino journey.

I am Facebook friends with Angel, but since I don't speak Spanish, it is mainly just keeping up with each other via Facebook posts and liking them to know we are still rooting for each other. I know that he has gone back to hike other sections of the Camino.

I have stayed in touch with Giacomo via the WhatsApp app. After returning from his Camino, he moved from Mallorca, Spain back to where his family lives in Florence, Italy. We chatted fairly often when I returned from my Camino, but then it dwindled to random chats around every six months. When I jumped back into writing my book, I let him know I was working on it again. He has continued to be my cheerleader, always rooting for me to finish my book. He is so sweet and it always makes me smile when I receive a message from him. Now we chat every few weeks to make sure the other person is still doing well and to let each other know that they are being thought of. I would love to go visit him in Italy, but the right time has not come. Maybe sometime in the future, we will meet again so he can show me his beautiful country and possibly even cook for me again. He holds a dear place in my heart and is a reminder of the friendships of the Camino. He is always there to remind me of my strength and determination when it wavers in me.

Since you are reading this, I obviously managed to also accomplish one more item on my bucket list. I published my first book! I was able to work through all the fears and figure out the self-publishing process. This opens me up to finally finish the book on our Hogs for Dogs ride and other books in the future! Stay tuned!

The walk on the Camino helped me to improve my self-esteem. It was one of the hardest things I had accomplished in my life, even though I had accomplished a lot of very difficult feats already. Not only was it a physical accomplishment, but it was also a mental one. I had to put mind over body to will myself to walk through the pain each day. I also had to tackle the mental challenge of walking day in and day out, especially through the dismal parts of the Meseta. It has given me the courage to deal with anything that comes my way. When confronted with something difficult, I now say to myself "Well, if you were able to walk the Camino, then you definitely can do this!" It pulled me out of a rut, made me look at my life, and pushed me to move forward with everything that I was afraid of before I left. It took a couple years for me to actually understand all of these changes. The strength from the Camino allowed me to experience life again and to be truly happy. The journey of the Camino gave me the tenacity, courage, and determination to accomplish anything that I set my mind to accomplish and provided the awareness that I have friends who will cheer me on along The Way!

The Journey Inward

Appendix A

This is a list of the items that I took on my hike. I feel like I did very well for my first hiking adventure. There are a few things that I would have done differently. I did not use the small notepad so I could have left that at home. My journal could have been lighter and with fewer pages. The second hiking shirt that I bought at Mast General was a bit too thick and it didn't always dry in time. My evening sandals could have been much lighter, but I bought a pair that I thought I could hike in if I needed to. I should have left the vitamins behind since they were so heavy. The can of sunscreen should have been smaller. All of this added extra weight that I could have done without.

I loved my Darn Tough socks and would highly recommend them! I was very happy that I took a shirt and a pair of long pants to wear in the evenings. It allowed me to wash both sets of walking shirts and shorts when we had a washer available. The long pants also kept me warm when the evenings were cool. I am grateful that I threw in my wind-resistant leggings at the last moment for those cold mornings that we had. Overall I was happy with what I brought with me and I never found that I was missing anything.

- Osprey Kestrel 48 backpack
- Black Diamond trekking poles

Janet Charbonneau

- Silk sleep sack
- Pillowcase
- Small inflatable fleece pillow
- Small light flannel blanket in a stuff sack
- One Small dry bag (for use in the shower area)
- One camping towel
- One small camping hand towel
- iPod with protective case and clip
- Earbuds
- Phone (texts, camera, web access, Facebook posts, WhatsApp app) with Otterbox case
- Levin solar charger
- Notebook for journal
- Small notebook for notes along the way
- Fanny pack (worn in front for easy access to phone, money, passport)
- Silk undercover money belt
- Sunglasses in silk cover that could be used to clean them
- Adapter and two cords(to charge the phone and solar charger)
- Two hiking shirts
- Two Columbia cargo hiking shorts
- Two sports bras
- Three pairs of underwear
- One short sleeve evening shirt
- One pair of evening pants
- One Under Armor long sleeve day or evening pullover shirt
- One pair of Keen sandals for the evening
- One pair of cheap flip-flops to wear in the shower
- One sports jacket
- One poncho
- One pair of black wind resistant leggings

The Journey Inward

- One Columbia extremely light white sun shirt
- One sarong/scarf
- One wide-brimmed hat
- Four pairs of Darn Tough socks
- Toiletries
- Vitamins
- Triple Flex supplements for knees
- Sunscreen
- Ziplocs
- Two rolls of camping toilet paper
- Roll of doggy pickup bags (in case I needed to carry used toilet paper off the trail)
- Clothespins
- Safety pins
- Lightweight camping rope
- Medical kit (band-aids, scissors, duct tape)
- Guidebook
- Headlamp
- Vivofit (worn on the wrist to capture step counts)

Janet Charbonneau

The Journey Inward

Order Your Custom Map Today!

My friend, Jay Schwantes, creates these incredible maps to commemorate your Camino journey, showing all your stops along The Way. He also has cool coffee mugs available with your route. Check them out at www.ARoadToSantiago.com.

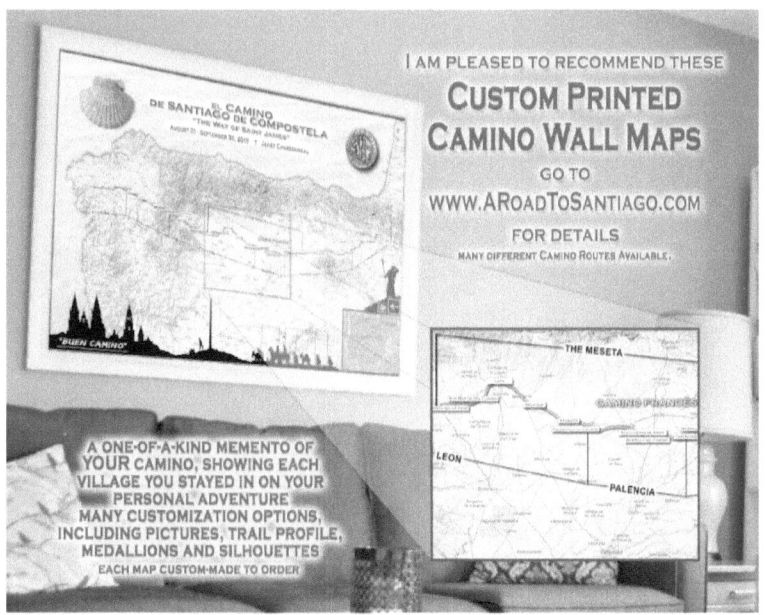

Janet Charbonneau

The Journey Inward

Thank you!

Dear Reader,

Thank you for joining me on my Camino journey. I hope you enjoyed the story and that it gave you the inspiration to follow your own dreams. Your inner strength is always there for you to discover.

If you loved the book and have a minute to spare, I would really appreciate a short review on the page or site where you bought the book. I believe in the power of word-of-mouth advertising, so your help in spreading the word is greatly appreciated. Reviews from readers like you make a huge difference in helping new readers discover the story of The Journey Inward.

Please join my Facebook page for future updates: www.Facebook.com/JanetCharbonneauAuthor

Thank you!

Janet Charbonneau

p.s. If you'd like to know when my next book comes out and want to receive occasional updates from me, then you can sign up for my newsletter on my website, TheJourneyInwardBook.com.

Janet Charbonneau

About the Author

Janet Charbonneau enjoys taking the road less traveled. Her adventures have included blue water cruising on a sailboat for four years and traveling all lower 48 states in seven months, riding a Harley-Davidson with her Golden Retriever, Bailey, in a sidecar. She hiked 440 miles on the Camino de Santiago as her latest adventure. By day, Janet is an IT Consultant and Account Manager, but she spends her nights writing about her adventures. Janet lives in Charleston, SC, with her Golden Retriever, Holly.

www.ingramcontent.com/pod-product-compliance
Lightning Source LLC
Chambersburg PA
CBHW020419010526
44118CB00010B/333